THE COMPLETE WOMEN'S EURO FINALS TOURNAMENTS 1984-2017

Marcel Haisma

British Library Cataloguing in Publication Data
A catalogue record for this book is available from the British Library

ISBN: 978-1-86223-393-5

Copyright © 2018, SOCCER BOOKS LIMITED (01472 696226)
72 St. Peter's Avenue, Cleethorpes, N.E. Lincolnshire, DN35 8HU, England
Web site   www.soccer-books.co.uk
e-mail   info@soccer-books.co.uk

All rights are reserved. No part of this publication may be reproduced, stored in a retrieval system or transmitted, in any form or by any means, electronic, mechanical, photocopying, recording, or otherwise, without the prior written permission of Soccer Books Limited.

Printed in the UK by 4edge Ltd.

AN INTRODUCTION TO THE UEFA WOMEN'S CHAMPIONSHIP

Although the first European Football Championship for men was organised by UEFA in 1958, the creation of a similar competition for women wasn't considered for many years. This is not perhaps surprising in view of the attitude to women's football in many countries for much of the 20th Century. In the present, it is hard to believe that the English Football Association only lifted a 50-year ban on women's teams playing on their members' pitches as late as 1971!

Unofficial women's European tournaments for national teams were held in Italy in 1969 and 1979 (won by Italy and Denmark respectively), but these were not organised under the auspices of UEFA so there was no formal international tournament until 1982 when the *UEFA European Competition for Representative Women's Teams* was launched. After three tournaments during the 1980s, the competition was given European Championship status by UEFA around 1990 and it has been held regularly since then.

Eight UEFA Women's Championships have taken place, preceded by the three editions of the European Competition for Representative Women's Teams and the tournament is now held every 4 years (earlier competitions were biennial). The 1984 Finals were won by Sweden, Norway won in 1987 and West Germany won in 1989, beginning an era of German domination. In the period from 1989 to 2013, the Germans (with a reunified team after 1990) won 7 out of 9 European titles, including 6 in a row between 1995 and 2013!

The tournament was initially held as a four team event and it wasn't until 1997 that it was expanded to eight teams. The third expansion came in 2009 with 12 participants and from 2017 onwards 16 teams compete for the championship. This book covers the matches played in each of these European finals tournaments since 1984 and complete and comprehensive statistics are included for each of the 185 finals games played during this period.

Two sister publications containing complete statistics for the men's UEFA European Football Championships from 1958 through to 2016 are also published by Soccer Books. These books include all qualification matches in addition to the finals matches.

UEFA EUROPEAN WOMEN'S CHAMPIONSHIP

EURO 1984

SEMI-FINALS

01.03.1984 Alexandra Stadium, Crewe: England – Denmark 2-1 (1-0).

ENGLAND: Linda CURL, Elisabeth DEIGHAN. (Coach: Martin REAGAN).

DENMARK: Gitte HANSEN, Charlotte NIELSEN-MANN, Glennie NIELSEN, Hanne PEDERSEN, Mette MUNK NIELSEN (57' Helle PEDERSEN), Susan MACKENSIE, Kirsten FABRIN, Pia ANDERSEN, Inge HINDKJAER, Annie GAM-PEDERSEN, Lone SMIDT NIELSEN. (Coach: Flemming SCHULTZ).

Referee: Kevin O'SULLIVAN (IRL)   Attendance: 1,000.

Goals: 31' Linda CURL 1-0, 49' Inge HINDKJAER 1-1, 51' Elisabeth DEIGHAN 2-1.

01.03.1984 Stadio Flaminio, Roma: Sweden – Italy 3-2 (1-2).

SWEDEN: Elisabeth LEIDINGE, Anette NICKLASSON, Angelica BUREVIK, Anette BÖRJESSON, Karin AHMAN-SVENSSON, Doris UUSITALO, Anna SVENJEBY, Mia KABERG-PETTERSSON, Eva ANDERSSON, Helen JOHANSSON, Pia SUNDHAGE. (Coach: Ulf LYFORS).

ITALY: Roberta RUSSO, Elisabetta SECCI (60' Viola LANGELLA), Maura FURLOTTI, Paola BONATO, Adele MARSILETTI, Maria MARIOTTI, Feriana FERRAGUZZI, Antonella CARTA (62' Ernesta VENUTO), Viviana BONTACCHIO, Elisabetta VIGNOTTO, Carolina MORACE. (Coach: Not known).

Referee: Werner FÖCKLER (GER)   Attendance: 5,000.

Goals: 18' Carolina MORACE 0-1, 21' Maura FURLOTTI 1-1 (og),
31' Elisabetta VIGNOTTO 1-2, 50' Pia SUNDHAGE 2-2, 59' Anette BÖRJESSON 3-2.

01.04.1984   Hjørring Stadion, Hjørring: Denmark – England 0-1 (0-1).

DENMARK: Gitte HANSEN, Charlotte NIELSEN-MANN, Glennie NIELSEN, Birgitte FREDERIKSEN (55' Annette MOGENSEN), Jette ANDERSEN, Hanne PEDERSEN, Hanne LARSEN (45' Pia ANDERSEN), Kirsten FABRIN, Lone SMIDT NIELSEN, Inge HINDKJAER, Annie GAM-PEDERSEN.   (Coach: Flemming SCHULTZ).

ENGLAND: Theresa WISEMAN, Linda CURL, Gillian COULTARD, Pat CHAPMAN, Deborah BAMPTON, Carol THOMAS-MCCUNE, Lorraine HANSON, Angela GALLIMORE, Elisabeth DEIGHAN, Kerry DAVIS, Morag PEARCE-KIRKLAND. (Coach: Martin REAGAN).

Referee: Kaj NATRI (FIN)   Attendance: 1,439.

Goal: 44' Deborah BAMPTON 0-1.

01.04.1984   Folkungavallen, Linköping: Italy – Sweden 1-2 (0-1).

ITALY: Roberta RUSSO, Maura FURLOTTI, Paola BONATO, Viviana BONTACCHIO, Anna MEGA, Adele MARSILETTI, Maria MARIOTTI, Viola LANGELLA, Feriana FERRAGUZZI, Elisabetta VIGNOTTO, Carolina MORACE.   (Coach: Not known).

SWEDEN: Elisabeth LEIDINGE (67' Inger ARNESSON), Karin AHMAN-SVENSSON, Angelica BUREVIK, Anette BÖRJESSON, Eva ANDERSSON (69' Anette NICKLASSON), Doris UUSITALO, Anna SVENJEBY, Mia KABERG-PETTERSSON, Ann JANSSON, Gunilla AXÉN, Pia SUNDHAGE.   (Coach: Ulf LYFORS).

Referee: Rolf HAUGEN (NOR)   Attendance: 5,162.

Goals: 26' Doris UUSITALO 0-1, 50' Carolina MORACE 1-1, 57' Pia SUNDHAGE 1-2.

FINAL

21.05.1984   Nya Ullevi, Göteborg: Sweden – England 1-0 (0-0).

SWEDEN: Elisabeth LEIDINGE, Anette HANSSON, Angelica BUREVIK, Anette BÖRJESSON, Eva ANDERSSON, Karin AHMAN-SVENSSON, Anna SVENJEBY, Mia KABERG-PETTERSSON, Ann JANSSON, Lena VIDEKULL, Pia SUNDHAGE. (Coach: Ulf LYFORS).

ENGLAND: Theresa WISEMAN, Morag PEARCE-KIRKLAND, Deborah BAMPTON, Gillian COULTARD (64' Tony BRIGHTWELL), Kerry DAVIS, Pat CHAPMAN (47' Janet TURNER), Linda CURL, Elisabeth DEIGHAN, Angela GALLIMORE, Lorraine HANSON, Carol THOMAS-MCCUNE. (Coach: Martin REAGAN).

Referee: Cornelius BAKKER (HOL)   Attendance: 5,552.

Goal: 57' Pia SUNDHAGE 1-0.

27.05.1984   Kenilworth Road, Luton: England – Sweden 1-0 (1-0, 1-0, 1-0).

ENGLAND: Theresa WISEMAN, Linda CURL, Kerry DAVIS, Deborah BAMPTON, Carol THOMAS, Elisabeth DEIGHAN, Gillian COULTARD, Pat CHAPMAN, Lorraine HANSON, Angela GALLIMORE, Morag PEARCE. (Coach: Martin REAGAN).

SWEDEN: Elisabeth LEIDINGE, Angelica BUREVIK, Anette BÖRJESSON, Eva ANDERSSON, Karin AHMAN-SVENSSON, Anna SVENJEBY, Mia KABERG-PETTERSSON, Ann JANSSON, Lena VIDEKULL (41' Doris UUSITALO), Pia SUNDHAGE, Helen JOHANSSON. (Coach: Ulf LYFORS).

Referee: Ignace GORIS (BEL)   Attendance: 2,567.

Goal: 31' Linda CURL 1-0.

Sweden won 4-3 on penalties to become European Champions.

Penalties: Linda CURL missed, Anette BÖRJESSON 0-1, Angela GALLIMORE 1-1, Eva ANDERSSON 1-2, Deborah BAMPTON 2-2, Helen JOHANSSON missed, Lorraine HANSON missed, Ann JANSSON 2-3, Kerry DAVIS 3-3, Pia SUNDHAGE 3-4.

UEFA EUROPEAN WOMEN'S CHAMPIONSHIP
EURO 1987

(The finals tournament was played in Norway)

SEMI-FINALS

11.06.1987   Ullevaal Stadion, Oslo: Norway – Italy 2-0 (1-0).

NORWAY: Janne ANDREASSEN, Heidi STØRE, Bjørg STORHAUG, Gunn NYBORG, Liv STRAEDET, Mariann KVISTNESS, Torill HOCH-NIELSEN, Tone HAUGEN, Trude STENDAL, Ellen SSCHEEL AALBU, Kari NIELSEN.   (Coach: Erling HOKSTAD).

ITALY: Roberta RUSSO, Maura FURLOTTI, Tiziana D'ORIO, Paola BONATO, Sandra PIERRAZZUOLI (53' Viviana BONTACCHIO), Marisa PERIN, Maria MARIOTTI, Feriana FERRAGUZZI, Antonella CARTA, Elisabetta VIGNOTTO, Ida GOLIN.
(Coach: Ettore RECAGNI).

Referee: Eysteinn GUDMUNDSSON (ISL)   Attendance: 5,154.

Goals: 40' Trude STENDAL 1-0, 73' Heidi STØRE 2-0.

11.06.1987   Melløs Stadion: Sweden – England 3-2 (1-1, 2-2).

SWEDEN: Elisabeth LEIDINGE, Anette BÖRJESSON, Eva ANDERSSON, Anette NICKLASSON, Gunilla AXÉN, Karin AHMAN-SVENSSON, Anna SVENJEBY (80' Marie KARLSSON), Helena CARLSSON, Lena VIDEKULL, Eleonor HULTIN (47' Helen JOHANSSON), Pia SUNDHAGE.   (Coach: Ulf LYFORS).

ENGLAND: Theresa WISEMAN, Linda CURL (5' Jane STANLEY / 41' Hope POWELL), Brenda SEMPARE, Sue LAW, Angela GALLIMORE, Kerry DAVIS, Gillian COULTARD, Deborah BAMPTON, Marie Anne SPACEY, Jackie SHERRARD, Jackie SLACK.
(Coach: Martin REAGAN).

Referee: Michal LISTKIEWICZ (POL)   Attendance: 300.

Goals: 1' Kerry DAVIS 0-1, 2' Anette BÖRJESSON 1-1, 89' Linda CURL 1-2, 90', 100' Gunilla AXÉN 2-2, 3-2.

3RD PLACE MATCH

13.06.1987   Marienlyst, Drammen: Italy – England 2-1 (2-1).

ITALY: Roberta RUSSO, Maura FURLOTTI, Marina CORDENONS, Paola BONATO, Antonella CARTA, Marisa PERIN, Maria MARIOTTI, Feriana FERRAGUZZI (45' FRIGERIO), Elisabetta VIGNOTTO, Carolina MORACE, Ida GOLIN (72' Sandra PIERAZZUOLI). (Coach: Ettore RECAGNI).

ENGLAND: Theresa WISEMAN, Sue LAW, Brenda SEMPARE, Angela GALLIMORE, Kerry DAVIS, Gillian COULTARD, Deborah BAMPTON, Marie Anne SPACEY, Jackie SHERRARD, Hope POWELL (69' Linda CURL), Lorraine HUNT. (Coach: Martin REAGAN).

Referee: Peter MIKKELSEN (DEN)   Attendance: 504.

Goals: 11' Kerry DAVIS 0-1, 36' Carolina MORACE 1-1, 45' Elisabetta VIGNOTTO 2-1.

FINAL

14.06.1987   Ullevaal Stadion, Oslo: Norway – Sweden 2-1 (1-0).

NORWAY: Janne ANDREASSEN, Heidi STØRE, Bjørg STORHAUG, Gunn NYBORG, Liv STRAEDET, Mariann KVISTNES, Torill HOCH-NIELSEN, Trude HAUGLAND, Trude STENDAL, Ellen SCHEEL AALBU, Kari NIELSEN (78' Hege LUDVIGSEN). (Coach: Erling HOKSTAD).

SWEDEN: Elisabeth LEIDINGE, Anette BÖRJESSON, Eva ANDERSSON, Anette NICKLASSON, Gunilla AXÉN, Karin AHMAN-SVENSSON, Anna SVENJEBY, Helena CARLSSON (41' Marie KARLSSON), Helen JOHANSSON (65' Anneli ANDELEN), Lena VIDEKULL, Pia SUNDHAGE.   (Coach: Ulf LYFORS).

Referee: Eere AHO (FIN)   Attendance: 8,470.

Goals: 28', 72' Trude STENDAL 1-0, 2-0, 73' Lena VIDEKULL 2-1.

Norway were European Champions

UEFA EUROPEAN WOMEN'S CHAMPIONSHIP
EURO 1989

(The finals tournament was played in Germany)

QUARTER-FINALS

15.10.1988   Odense Stadium, Odense: Denmark – Sweden 1-5 (0-3).

DENMARK: Helle BJERREGAARD, Karina SEFRON, Annette MOGENSEN, Bonny MADSEN, Jannie HANSEN, Mette BACH KJAER, Pernilla OBEL, Marianne JACOBSEN (71' Helle JENSEN), Lone SMIDT NIELSEN, Lisbeth PEDERSEN (43' Annette TYCHOSEN), Annie GAM-PEDERSEN.   (Coach: Keld GANTZHORN).

SWEDEN: Elisabeth LEIDINGE, Anette HANSSON, Eva ZEIKFALVY, Ane LUNDIN-BORGWALL, Eva KÄRRBERG, Marie KARLSSON, Ingid JOHANSSON, Anneli ANDELEN, Lena VIDEKULL, Helen JOHANSSON, Pia SUNDHAGE. (Coach: Not known).

Referee: Gudmundur HARALDSSON (ISL)   Attendance: 375.

Goals: 2', 29' Lena VIDEKULL 0-1, 0-2, 40' Pia SUNDHAGE 0-3, 51' Lone SMIDT NIELSEN 1-3, 75' Anette HANSSON 1-4, 81' Anneli ANDELEN 1-5.

22.10.1988   Lystlunden, Horten: Norway – Netherlands 2-1 (2-0).

NORWAY: Hege LUDVIGSEN, Bjørg STORHAUG, Gunn NYBORG, Tone HAUGEN, Cathrine ZABOROWSKI, Liv STRAEDET, Torill HOCH-NIELSEN, Birthe HEGSTAD, Sissel GRUDE, Turid STORHAUG, Linda MEDALEN.   (Coach: Erling HOKSTAD).

NETHERLANDS: Lies KOLS, Jannie TIMISELA, Anet SMITS, Danielle DE WINTER, ZWARTS, Ria VESTJENS, Tilly VAN ROOYEN-BONTE, Thea VAN ERP, Sarina WIEGMAN, Marjoke DE BAKKER, Regina VAN MILTENBURG.   (Coach: Piet BUTER).

Referee: Wolf-Günter WIESEL (GER)   Attendance: 623.

Goals: 10' Sissel GRUDE 1-0, 15' Turid STORHAUG 2-0, 53' Marjoke DE BAKKER 2-1.

26.10.1988 Ryavallen, Boras: Sweden – Denmark 1-1 (1-1).

SWEDEN: Elisabeth LEIDINGE, Anette HANSSON, Eva ZEIKFALVY (71' Tina NILSSON), Ane LUNDIN-BORGWALL, Eva KÄRRBERG (41' Camilla NEPTUNE), Marie KARLSSON, Ingrid JOHANSSON, Anneli ANDELEN, Lena VIDEKULL, Helen JOHANSSON, Pia SUNDHAGE. (Coach: Not known).

DENMARK: Helle BJERREGAARD, Karina SEFRON, Jannie HANSEN, Sus MOGENSEN (7' Linda THOMSEN), Alice LARSEN, Marianne JACOBSEN, Lotte BAGGE, Annie GAM-PEDERSEN, Annette TYCHOSEN, Lone SMIDT NIELSEN, Helle JENSEN (62' Mette BACH KJAER). (Coach: Keld GANTZHORN).

Referee: Eere AHO (FIN) Attendance: 595.

Goals: 2' Lena VIDEKULL 1-0, 16' Lotte BAGGE 1-1.

06.11.1988 Sportpark Rijsoord, Rijsoord: Netherlands – Norway 0-3 (0-1).

NETHERLANDS: Lies KOLS, Jannie TIMISELA, Anet SMITS, Danielle DE WINTER, ZWARTS, Ria VESTJENS, Tilly VAN ROOYEN-BONTE, Thea VAN ERP, Sarina WIEGMAN, Marjoke DE BAKKER, Regina VAN MILTENBURG. (Coach: Piet BUTER).

NORWAY: Hege LUDVIGSEN, Bjørg STORHAUG, Gunn NYBORG, Tone HAUGEN, Cathrine ZABOROWSKI, Liv STRAEDET, Heidi STØRE, Linda MEDALEN, Birthe HEGSTAD (41' Agnete CARLSEN), Sissel GRUDE, Turid STORHAUG. (Coach: Erling HOKSTAD).

Referee: John LLOYD (WAL) Attendance: 1,500.

Goals: 38' Sissel GRUDE 0-1, 57' Turid STORHAUG 0-2, 79' Agnete CARLSEN 0-3.

06.11.1988 Stadio Giglio, Reggio Emilia: Italy – France 2-0 (2-0).

ITALY: Roberta RUSSO, Paola BONATO, Elisabetta BAVAGNOLI (58' Antonella CARTA), Elisabetta SALDI, Anna MEGA, Adele MARSILETTI, Maria MARIOTTI, Feriana FERRAGUZZI, Federica D'ASTOLFO (70' PRINCIPE), Carolina MORACE, Elisabetta VIGNOTTO. (Coach: Sergio GUENZA).

FRANCE: Sylvie JOSSET, Veronique NOWAK, Marie-Angele BLIN, Marie-Christine UMDENSTOCK, Nathalie TARADE, Sophie RYCKEBOER-CHARRIER, Elisabeth LOISEL, Corinne ERNOULT (41' Cécile MARGARIA), Isabelle MUSSET, Regine MISMARCQ, Veronique ROMAGNOLI. (Coach: Aimé MIGNOT).

Referee: Charles AGIUS (MLT) Attendance: 3,000.

Goals: 14', 44' Carolina MORACE 1-0, 2-0.

26.11.1988   Venue not recorded: Czechoslovakia – Germany 1-1 (1-0).

CZECHOSLOVAKIA: Milada NOVOTNA, Eva HANIAKOVÁ, Jaroslava FARMAKOVA, Martina JEDLICKOVÁ, Zdena CHALUPKOVA, Hana TRICARICOOVA, Marie TLACHOVA, Dagmar PROCHAZKOVA, Jana PALETTIOVA, NOVÁKOVÁ, BULIROVA. (Coach: Not known).

GERMANY: Marion ISBERT, Sissy RAITH, Britta UNSLEBER, Jutta NARDENBACH, Petra LANDERS, Petra DAMM (63' Doris FISCHEN), Martina VOSS-TECKLENBURG, Claudia SONN, Silvia NEID, Heidi MOHR, Thekla KRAUE (24' Roswitha BINDL). (Coach: Gero BISANZ).

Referee: Ion CRACIUNESCU (ROM)   Attendance: 5,000.

Goals: 21' NOVÁKOVÁ 1-0, 49' Roswitha BINDL 1-1.

11.12.1988   Stade de Vallauris, Vallauris: France – Italy 1-2 (1-0).

FRANCE: Sylvie JOSSET (52' Sandrine ROUX), Marie-Christine UMDENSTOCK, Nathalie TARADE, Sophie RYCKEBOER-CHARRIER, Catherine MERCADIER, Marie-Angele BLIN, Martine PUENTES (75' Cécile MARGARIA), Elisabeth LOISEL, Veronique ROMAGNOLI, Isabelle MUSSET, Regine MISMARCQ.   (Coach: Aimé MIGNOT).

ITALY: Roberta RUSSO, Paola BONATO, Elisabetta BAVAGNOLI, Elisabetta SALDI, Anna MEGA, Adele MARSILETTI, Maria MARIOTTI, Feriana FERRAGUZZI, Federica D'ASTOLFO, Elisabetta VIGNOTTO, Carolina MORACE.   (Coach: Sergio GUENZA).

Referee: José SILVA (POR)   Attendance: 2,100.

Goals: 3' Isabelle MUSSET 1-0, 66', 72' Carolina MORACE 1-1, 1-2.

17.12.1988   Fritz-Walter-Stadion, Kaiserslautern:
                                    Germany – Czechoslovakia 2-0 (1-0).

GERMANY: Marion ISBERT, Sissy RAITH, Britta UNSLEBER, Jutta NARDENBACH, Petra LANDERS, Roswitha BINDL, Angelika FEHRMANN (71' Doris FITSCHEN), Martina VOSS-TECKLENBURG, Claudia SONN (74' Petra DAMM), Silvia NEID, Heidi MOHR. (Coach: Gero BISANZ).

CZECHOSLOVAKIA: Milada NOVOTNA, Eva HANIAKOVÁ, Jaroslava FARMAKOVA, HDLIKOVA (29' Iveta HEKELOVA), Zdena CHALUPKOVA, Jana PALETTIOVA, Hana TRICARICOOVA, Marie TLACHOVA, Dagmar PROCHAZKOVA, NOVÁKOVÁ, BULIROVA. (Coach: Not known).

Referee: Charles GILSON (LUX)   Attendance: 2,053.

Goals: 26' Silvia NEID 1-0, 55' Heidi MOHR 2-0.

SEMI-FINALS

28.06.1989 Leimbachstadion, Siegen: Germany – Italy 1-1 (0-0, 1-1, 1-1).

GERMANY: Marion ISBERT, Sissy RAITH, Jutta NARDENBACH, Petra LANDERS, Frauke KUHLMANN, Martina VOSS-TECKLENBURG, Ursula LOHN (56' Roswitha BINDL), Doris FITSCHEN, Petra DAMM, Silvia NEID (100' Angelika FEHRMANN), Heid MOHR. (Coach: Gero BISANZ).

ITALY: Roberta RUSSO, Paola BONATO, Elisabetta SALDI, Emma IOZZELLI, Anna MEGA (69' Elisabetta BAVAGNOLI / 100' Federica D'ASTOLFO), Adele MARSILETTI, Maria MARIOTTI, Feriana FERRAGUZZI, Antonella CARTA, Elisabetta VIGNOTTO, Carolina MORACE. (Coach: Sergio GUENZA).

Referee: Brian HILL (ENG) Attendance: 8,000.

Goals: 57' Silvia NEID 1-0, 72' Elisabetta VIGNOTTO 1-1.

Germany won 4-3 on penalties.

Penalties: Martina VOSS-TECKLENBURG missed, Feriana FERRAGUZZI 0-1, Frauke KUHLMANN 1-1, Antonella CARTA missed, Roswitha BINDL 2-1, Carolina MORACE 2-2, Doris FITSCHEN 3-2, Elisabetta VIGNOTTO missed, Angelika FEHRMANN missed, Federica D'ASTOLFO 3-3, Petra LANDERS missed, Emma IOZZELLI missed, Marion ISBERT 4-3, Adele MARSILETTI missed.

28.06.1989 Nattenberg Stadion, Lüdenscheid, Lüdenscheid:
Norway – Sweden 2-1 (1-0).

NORWAY: Hege LUDVIGSEN, Trine STENBERG, Gunn NYBORG, Heidi STØRE, Torill HOCH-NIELSEN (85' Turid STORHAUG), Tone HAUGEN, Cathrine ZABOROWSKI (75' Agnete CARLSEN), Liv STRAEDET, Linda MEDALEN, Birthe HEGSTAD, Sissel GRUDE. (Coach: Erling HOKSTAD).

SWEDEN: Elisabeth LEIDINGE, Anette HANSSON, Eva ZEIKFALVY (41' Pia SYREN), Camilla FORS, Marie KARLSSON, Ingrid JOHANSSON, Asa PERSSON (41' Eleonor HULTIN), Helen JOHANSSON, Anneli ANDELEN, Lena VIDEKULL, Pia SUNDHAGE. (Coach: Not known).

Referee: Cornelius BAKKER (HOL) Attendance: 2,500.

Goals: 2' Linda MEDALEN 1-0, 53' Sissel GRUDE 2-0, 54' Lena VIDEKULL 2-1.

3RD PLACE MATCH

30.06.1989 Stadion an der Bremer Brücke, Osnabrück: Sweden – Italy 2-1 (1-1).

SWEDEN: Elisabeth LEIDINGE, Anette HANSSON, Camilla FORS (41' Anneli ANDELEN), Pia SYREN, Malin SWEDBERG, Camilla NEPTUNE, Marie KARLSSON, Ingird JOHANSSON, Helen JOHANSSON, Eleonor HULTIN (41' Lena VIDEKULL), Pia SUNDHAGE. (Coach: Not known).

ITALY: Roberta RUSSO, Paola BONATO, Elisabetta SALDI, Emma IOZZELLI, Anna MEGA, Elisabetta BAVAGNOLI, Adele MARSILETTI, Maria MARIOTTI, Feriana FERRAGUZZI, Antonella CARTA (52' Federica D'ASTOLFO), Carolina MORACE. (Coach: Sergio GUENZA).

Referee: Ivan GREGR (CZE)   Attendance: 2,500.

Goals: 27' Feriana FERRAGUZZI 0-1, 43' Pia SUNDHAGE 1-1, 100' Helen JOHANSSON 2-1.

Sweden won following extra time.

FINAL

02.07.1989 Stadion an der Bremer Brücke, Osnabrück:
  Germany – Norway 4-1 (3-0).

GERMANY: Marion ISBERT, Sissy RAITH, Jutta NARDENBACH, Frauke KUHLMANN, Andrea HABERLASS (27' Roswitha BINDL), Martina VOSS-TECKLENBURG, Ursula LOHN, Doris FITSCHEN (62' Angelika FEHRMANN), Petra DAMM, Silvia NEID, Heidi MOHR. (Coach: Gero BISANZ).

NORWAY: Hege LUDVIGSEN, Gunn NYBORG, Heidi STØRE, Torill HOCH-NIELSEN (41' Turid STORHAUG), Cathrine ZABOROWSKI, Liv STRAEDET, Tone HAUGEN, Agnete CARLSEN, Linda MEDALEN, Birthe HEGSTAD (67' Trude HAUGLAND), Sissel GRUDE. (Coach: Erling HOKSTAD).

Referee: Carlos VALENTE (POR)   Attendance: 22,000.

Goals: 22', 36' Ursula LOHN 1-0, 2-0, 45' Heidi MOHR 3-0, 54' Sissel GRUDE 3-1, 73' Angelika FEHRMANN 4-1.

Norway were European Champions

UEFA EUROPEAN WOMEN'S CHAMPIONSHIP EURO 1991

(The finals tournament was played in Denmark)

QUARTER-FINALS

14.11.1990   Kristiansand, Stadion, Kristiansand: Norway – Hungary 2-1 (0-0).

NORWAY: Reidun SETH, Tina SVENSSON, Heidi STØRE, Trine STENBERG, Gunn NYBORG (41' Ann-Kristin AARONES), Cathrine ZABOROWSKI (41' Lisberth BAKKEN), Liv STRAEDET, Hege RIISE, Tone HAUGEN, Agnete CARLSEN, Birthe HEGSTAD. (Coach: Even PELLERUD).

HUNGARY: Mária KISS, Judith TÓTH, Tünde NAGY, Lászlóné KISS, Beata FŰLŐP, PAPP, Agnes BÁRFY, Anikó KEREKES-BILICSNE, Eva SZARKA, Edit KERN, Timea FŐFAI. (Coach: Not known).

Referee: Michal LISTKIEWICZ (POL)   Attendance: 808.

Goals: 65' Hege RIISE 1-0, 74' Trine STENBERG 2-0, 80' Edit KERN 2-1.

18.11.1990   Malmö Stadion, Malmö: Sweden – Italy 1-1 (1-1).

SWEDEN: Ing-Marie OLSSON, Eva ZEIKFALVY, Malin LUNDGREN, Malin SWEDBERG (41' Eleonor HULTIN), Malin STALKLINT, Asa LINDQVIST, Marie KARLSSON, Susanne HEDBERG, Lena VIDEKULL (41' Anneli ANDELEN), Helen JOHANSSON, Pia SUNDHAGE. (Coach: Not known).

ITALY: Stefania ANTONINI, Raffaela SALMASO, Elisabetta SALDI, Emma IOZZELLI, Paola BONATO, Elisabetta BAVAGNOLI, Adele MARSILETTI, Feriana FERRAGUZZI, Antonella CARTA, Carolina MORACE, Anna Maria MIGLIACCIO. (Coach: Sergio GUENZA).

Referee: Klaus PESCHEL (GER)   Attendance: 450.

Goals: 19' Pia SUNDHAGE 1-0, 43' Antonella CARTA 1-1.

24.11.1990   Vejle Stadion, Vejle: Denmark – Netherlands 0-0.

DENMARK: Helle BJERREGAARD, Karina SEFRON, Helle ROTBOLL, Jannie HANSEN, Ulla CHRISTENSEN, Lisbet KOLDING, Marianne JENSEN, Lotte BAGGE, Annette TYCHOSEN (41' Alice LARSEN), Helle JENSEN (41' Tina JENSEN), Annia GAM-PEDERSEN. (Coach: Keld GANTZHORN).

NETHERLANDS: Marleen WISSINK, Margriet LIMBEEK, Hesterine DE REUS, Ria VESTJENS, Jannie TIMISELA, THOMASSEN, Anet SMITS, Nathalie GEERIS, Mildred BAAL, Anne VAN WAARDEN, Marjoke DE BAKKER. (Coach: Bert VAN LINGEN).

Referee: Rodger GIFFORD (WAL)   Attendance: 250.

25.11.1990   Adams Park, Wycombe: England – Germany 1-4 (1-3).

ENGLAND: Theresa WISEMAN, Louise WALLER, Brenda SEMPARE, Gillian COULTARD, Marie Anne SPACEY, Jackie SHERRARD, Janice MURRAY, Clare LAMBERT, Kerry DAVIS, Karen WALKER, Jackie SLACK. (Coach: Not known).

GERMANY: Marion ISBERT, Roswitha BINDL, Sissy RAITH, Britta UNSLEBER, Jutta NARDENBACH, Martina VOSS-TECKLENBURG (67' Gudrun GOTTSCHLICH), Ursula LOHN, Doris FITSCHEN, Petra DAMM (50' Bettina WIEGMANN), Heidi MOHR, Silvia NEID. (Coach: Gero BISANZ).

Referee: Jaap UILENBERG (HOL)   Attendance: 2,000.

Goals: 18' Heidi MOHR 0-1, 28' Karen WALKER 1-1, 34' Ursula LOHN 1-2, 37', 54' Heidi MOHR 1-3, 1-4.

25.11.1990   Venue not recorded: Hungary – Norway 0-2 (0-1).

HUNGARY: Mária KISS, Ildikó NAGYABONYI, Tünde NAGY, Lászlóné KISS, Beata FÜLÖP, PAPP, Agnes BÁRFY, Anikó KEREKES-BILICSNE, Eva SZARKA, Edit KERN, Timea FŐFAI. (Coach: Not known).

NORWAY: Reidun SETH, Tina SVENSSON, Heidi STØRE, Trine STENBERG, Gunn NYBORG (41' Cathrine ZABOROWSKI), Liv STRAEDET, Hege RIISE, Tone HAUGEN, Agnete CARLSEN, Lisbeth BAKKEN, Birthe HEGSTAD (41' Linda MEDALEN). (Coach: Even PELLERUD).

Referee: Karl-Josef ASSENMACHER (GER)   Attendance: 400.

Goals: 20' Tone HAUGEN 0-1, 75' Lisbeth BAKKEN 0-2.

08.12.1990   Romeo Menti, Castellammare di Stabia: Italy – Sweden 0-0.

ITALY: Stefania ANTONINI, Raffaela SALMASO, Elisabetta SALDI, Emma IOZZELLI (68' Giorgia BRENZAN), Paola BONATO, Elisabetta BAVAGNOLI, Adele MARSILETTI, Feriana FERRAGUZZI, Antonella CARTA, Carolina MORACE, Anna Maria MIGLIACCIO. (Coach: Sergio GUENZA).

SWEDEN: Elisabeth LEIDINGE, Eva ZEIKFALVY, Malin LUNDGREN, Pia SYREN, Malin SWEDBERG, Asa LINDQVIST, Marie KARLSSON (41' Malin STALKLINT), Susanne HEDBERG, Lena VIDEKULL, Anneli ANDELEN, Pia SUNDHAGE. (Coach: Not known).

Referee: Guy GOETHALS (BEL)   Attendance: 4,000.

Yellow Cards: Paola BONATO, Antonella CARTA (ITA), Malin STALKLINT (SWE).

Red card: 67' Stafania ANTONINI (ITA).

08.12.1990   Denekamp Stadion, Denekamp: Netherlands – Denmark 0-0 (0-0, 0-0).

NETHERLANDS: Marleen WISSINK, Margriet LIMBEEK, Hesterine DE REUS, Ria VESTJENS, Jannie TIMISELA, THOMASSEN, Anet SMITS, Nathalie GEERIS, Mildred BAAL, Anne VAN WAARDEN, Marjoke DE BAKKER. (Coach: Bert VAN LINGEN).

DENMARK: Helle BJERREGAARD, Karina SEFRON, Helle ROTBOLL, Jannie HANSEN, Ulla CHRISTENSEN, Irene STELLING (41' Tina JENSEN), Lisbet KOLDING, Marianne JENSEN, Lotte BAGGE, Helle JENSEN (41' Marianne JACOBSEN), Annie GAM-PEDERSEN. (Coach: Keld GANTZHORN).

Referee: Andrew WADDELL (SCO)   Attendance: 3,500.

Goal: 100' Helen ROTBOLLl 0-1.

Yellow Cards: Anet SMITS (NET), Helle BJERREGAARD, Helle ROTBOLL, Lotte BAGGE.

Denmark won following extra time.

16.12.1990   Ruhrstadion, Bochum: Germany – England 2-0 (1-0).

GERMANY: Marion ISBERT, Britta UNSLEBER, Dagmar UEBELHŐR (53' Susanne BRÜCK), Jutta NARDENBACH, Roswitha BINDL, Sissy RAITH, Martina VOSS-TECKLENBURG, Ursula LOHN (63' Bettina WIEGMANN), Doris FITSCHEN, Silvia NEID, Heidi MOHR. (Coach: Gero BISANZ).

ENGLAND: Theresa WISEMAN, Louise WALLER, Brenda SEMPARE, Clare TAYLOR, Gillian COULTARD, Marie Anne SPACEY, Jackie SHERRARD, Janice MURRAY, Clare LAMBERT, Kerry DAVIS, Karen WALKER. (Coach: Not known).

Referee: Michel GIRARD (FRA)   Attendance: 3,051.

Goals: 24', 80' Britta UNSLEBER 1-0, 2-0.

SEMI-FINALS

10.07.1991   Hjørring Stadion, Hjørring: Norway – Denmark 0-0.

NORWAY: Reidun SETH, Tina SVENSSON, Heidi STØRE, Gunn NYBORG, Cathrine ZABOROWSKI, Liv STRAEDET (52' Margunn HUMLESTØL), Hege RIISE, Gro ESPESETH, Agnete CARLSEN, Linda MEDALEN, Birthe HEGSTAD.
(Coach: Even PELLERUD)
Sub: Ann-Kristin AARONES.

DENMARK: Helle BJERREGAARD, Karina SEFRON, Bonny MADSEN, Jannie HANSEN, Ulla CHRISTENSEN, Pernille OBEL (49' Annette TYCHOSEN), Lisbet KOLDING, Marianne JENSEN, Lotte BAGGE, Helle JENSEN (59' Marianne JACOBSEN), Annie GAM-PEDERSEN. (Coach: Keld GANTZHORN).

Referee: Luben SPASOV (BUL)   Attendance: 4,850.

Norway won 8-7 on penalties.

Penalties: Tina SVENSSON 1-0, Lisbet KOLDING 1-1, Ann-Kristin AARONES missed, Annette TYCHOSEN 1-2, Agnete CARLSEN 2-2, Karina SEFRON 2-3, Cathrine ZABOROWSKI 3-3, Marianne JACOBSEN missed, Hege RIISE 4-3, Lotte BAGGE 4-4, Linda MEDALEN 5-4, Annie GAM-PEDERSEN 5-5, Birthe HEGSTAD 6-5, Ulla CHRISTENSEN 6-6, Gunn NYBORG 7-6, Jannie HANSEN 7-7, Gro ESPESETH 8-7, Marianne JENSEN missed.

11.07.1991   Frederikshavn Stadion, Frederikshavn: Germany – Italy 3-0 (1-0).

GERMANY: Marion ISBERT, Britta UNSLEBER, Sissy RAITH (67' Sandra HENGST), Jutta NARDENBACH, Frauke KUHLMANN, Doris FITSCHEN, Petra DAMM, Bettina WIEGMANN, Martina VOSS-TECKLENBURG (64' Gudrun GOTTSCHLICH), Silvia NEID, Heidi MOHR.   (Coach: Gero BISANZ).

ITALY: Giorgia BRENZAN, Paola BONATO, Elisabetta BAVAGNOLI., Elisabetta SALDI, Emma IOZZELLI (30' Silvia FIORINI), Maura FURLOTTI, Adele MARSILETTI, Feriana FERRAGUZZI, Antonella CARTA, Carolina MORACE, Anna Maria MIGLIACCIO (43' Federica D'ASTOLFO).   (Coach: Sergio GUENZA).

Referee: Roger PHILIPPI (LUX)   Attendance: 3,000.

Goals: 30', 58' Heidi MOHR 1-0, 2-0, 60' Sissy RAITH 3-0.

3RD PLACE MATCH

14.07.1991   Aalborg Stadion, Aalborg: Denmark – Italy 2-1 (1-0, 1-1).

DENMARK: Helle BJERREGAARD, Karina SEFRON, Bonny MADSEN, Jannie HANSEN, Irene STELLING, Lisbet KOLDING, Marianne JENSEN, Lotte BAGGE, Annette TYCHOSEN, Helle JENSEN (54' Pernille OBEL), Annie GAM-PEDERSEN (60' Mette NIELSEN).   (Coach: Keld GANTZHORN).

ITALY: Giorgia BRENZAN, Paola BONATO, Elisabetta BAVAGNOLI., Elisabetta SALDI (41' Emma IOZZELLI), Maura FURLOTTI, Marina CORDENONS, Adele MARSILETTI, Silvia FIORINI, Feriana FERRAGUZZI, Antonella CARTA (46' Federica D'ASTOLFO), Carolina MORACE.   (Coach: Sergio GUENZA).

Referee: Garcia DE LOZA (ESP)   Attendance: 3,100.

Goals: 22' Helle JENSEN 1-0, 69' Silvia FIORINI 1-1, 100' Bonny MADSEN 2-1.

Yellow Card: Annette TYCHOSEN (DEN).

Red card: Federica D'ASTOLFO (ITA).

Denmark won following extra time.

FINAL

14.07.1991   <u>Aalborg Stadion, Aalborg</u>: Germany – Norway 3-1 (0-0, 1-1).

GERMANY: Marion ISBERT, Britta UNSLEBER (52' Gudrun GOTTSCHLICH), Sissy RAITH, Jutta NARDENBACH, Frauke KUHLMANN, Bettina WIEGMANN, Martina VOSS-TECKLENBURG (100' Katja BORNSCHEIN), Doris FITSCHEN, Petra DAMM, Silvia NEID, Heidi MOHR. (Coach: Gero BISANZ).

NORWAY: Reidun SETH, Tina SVENSSON, Heidi STØRE (100' Margunn HUMLESTØL), Gunn NYBORG, Cathrine ZABOROWSKI, Liv STRAEDET (70' Ann-Kristin AARONES), Hege RIISE, Gro ESPESETH, Agnete CARLSEN, Linda MEDALEN, Birthe HEGSTAD. (Coach: Even PELLERUD).

Referee: James MCCLUSKEY (SCO)   Attendance: 6,000.

Goals: 54' Birthe HEGSTAD 0-1, 62', 100' Heidi MOHR 1-1, 2-1, 110' Silvia NEID 3-1.

Germany were European Champions

UEFA EUROPEAN WOMEN'S CHAMPIONSHIP
EURO 1993

(The finals tournament was played in Italy)

QUARTER-FINALS

10.10.1992   Ullevaal, Stadion, Oslo: Norway – Netherlands 3-0 (0-0).

NORWAY: Bente NORDBY, Tina SVENSSON (78' Gunn NYBORG), Heidi STØRE, Hege RIISE, Elin KROKAN, Gro ESPESETH, Agnete CARLSEN, Ann-Kristin AARONES, Cathrine ZABOROWSKI, Linda MEDALEN (70' Ase Iren STEINE), Birthe HEGSTAD. (Coach: Even PELLERUD).

NETHERLANDS: Marleen WISSINK, Margriet LIMBEEK, Christa BOUW, Marjon VAN DE PLOEG, Jannie TIMISELA, Linda SCHOONOORD, Sandra KEEREWEER, Nathalie GEERIS, Regina VAN MILTENBURG, Saskia VAN DE VELDE, Miranda VERRIPS. (Coach: Jan DERKS).

Referee: Nemus DJURHUUS (FRO)   Attendance: 695.

Goals: 49' Birthe HEGSTAD 1-0, 53' Hege RIISE 2-0, 61' Elin KROKAN 3-0.

Yellow Cards: Linda SCHOONOORD, Sandra KEEREWEER (NET).

11.10.1992   Eduard Streltsov, Moskva: Russia – Germany 0-7 (0-5).

RUSSIA: Svetlana PETKO, Marina BURAKOVA, Natalia BUNDUKI, Valentina BARKOVA, Ludmilla KOROBITSYNA, Elena KONONOVA, KOUTCHER, KONIAKOVA, Irina GRIGORIEVA, Tatiana EGOROVA, Elena SOTNIKOVA.   (Coach: Not known).

GERMANY: Elke WALTHER, Britta UNSLEBER, Dagmar POHLMANN (41' Katja BORNSCHEIN), Anouschka BERNHARD, Susanne BRÜCK, Bettina WIEGMANN, Martina VOSS-TECKLENBURG, Doris FITSCHEN, Heidi MOHR, Patricia BROCKER (58' Maren MEINERT), Silvia NEID.   (Coach: Gero BISANZ).

Referee: Daniel RODUIT (SUI)   Attendance: 500.

Goals: 5' Martina VOSS-TECKLENBURG 0-1, 16' Silvia NEID 0-2, 17' Martina VOSS-TECKLENBURG 0-3, 19' Britta UNSLEBER 0-4, 42' Patricia BROCKER 0-5, 71' Heidi MOHR 0-6, 79' Britta UNSLEBER 0-7.

Yellow Card: Ludmilla KOROBITSYNA (RUS).

13.10.1992   Ryavallen, Boras: Sweden – Denmark 1-2 (1-1).

SWEDEN: Elisabeth LEIDINGE, Malin LUNDGREN, Asa JAKOBSSON, Kristin BENGTSSON, Camilla NEPTUNE (60' Susanne HEDBERG), Annika LARSSON, Lena VIDEKULL, Helen NILSSON, Ulrika KALTE, Helen JOHANSSON (75' Malin SWEDBERG), Anneli ANDELEN.   (Coach: Not known).

DENMARK: Helle BJERREGAARD, Karina SEFRON, Bonny MADSEN, Irene STELLING, Janne RASMUSSEN, Susan MACKENSIE, Lisbet KOLDING, Rikke HOLM, Lotte BAGGE, Hanne NISSEN, Helle JENSEN (80' Marianne JENSEN).   (Coach: Keld GANTZHORN).

Referee: Wojciech RUDY (POL)   Attendance: 393.

Goals: 10' Anneli ANDELEN 1-0, 14' Janne RASMUSSEN 1-1, 78' Helle JENSEN 1-2.

Yellow Cards: Lena VIDEKULL (SWE), Lisbet KOLDING (DEN).

17.10.1992   Comunale Solofra, Solofra: Italy – England 3-2 (2-0).

ITALY: Giorgia BRENZAN, Raffaela SALMASO, Dolores PRESTFILLIPPO, Emma IOZZELLI, Marina CORDENONS, Elisabetta BAVAGNOLI, Adele MARSILETTI, Silvia FIORINI, Federica D 'ASTOLFO, Antonella CARTA, Carolina MORACE.
(Coach: Sergio GUENZA).

ENGLAND: Tracey DAVIDSON, Louise WALLER, Clare TAYLOR, Samantha BRITTON, Marie Anne SPACEY, Jackie SHERRARD, Janice MURRAY, Kerry DAVIS, Gillian COULTARD, Karen WALKER, Gail BORMAN.   (Coach: Not known).

Referee: Gilles VEISSIÈRE (FRA)   Attendance: Not known

Goals: 37', 40' Carolina MORACE 1-0, 2-0, 54' Silvia FIORINI 3-0, 73' Karen WALKER 3-1, 79' Marie-Anne SPACEY 3-2.

Yellow Cards: Federica D'ASTOLFO, Carolina MORACE (ITA), Samantha BRITTON (ENG).

07.11.1992   Sportpark Tijenraan, Raalte: Netherlands – Norway 0-3 (0-2).

NETHERLANDS: Marleen WISSINK, Margriet LIMBEEK, Ingrid KLOMP, Sandra VAN TOL, Nathalie GEERIS, Marjon VAN DE PLOEG, Jannie TIMISELA, Linda SCHOONOORD, Miranda NOOM, Regina VAN MILTENBURG, Saskia VAN DE VELDE. (Coach: Frans DERKS).

NORWAY: Reidun SETH, Tina SVENSSON, Heidi STØRE, Hege RIISE, Elin KROKAN, Gro ESPESETH (62' Anne Nymark RYLANDSHOLM), , Agnete CARLSEN, Ann-Kristin AARONES (56' Ase Iren STEINE), Cathrine ZABOROWSKI, Linda MEDALEN, Birthe HEGSTAD.   (Coach: Even PELLERUD).

Referee: Gerd GRABHER (AUT)   Attendance: 1,500.

Goals: 30' Hege RIISE 0-1, 37' Linda MEDALEN 0-2, 52' Tina SVENSSON 0-3.

Yellow Cards: Marleen WISSINK (NET), Gro ESPESETH (NOR).

07.11.1992   Hjørring Stadion, Hjørring: Denmark – Sweden 1-1 (1-1).

DENMARK: Helle BJERREGAARD, Karina SEFRON, Bonny MADSEN, Irene STELLING, Janne RASMUSSEN, Susan MACKENSIE, Lisbet KOLDING, Rikke HOLM, Lotte BAGGE, Hanne NISSEN, Marianne JENSEN.   (Coach: Keld GANTZHORN)..

SWEDEN: Elisabeth LEIDINGE, Malin LUNDGREN, Asa JAKOBSSON, Eva ZEIKFALVY, Malin SWEDBERG (41' Susanne HEDBERG), Annika LARSSON, Anna WÄLLERSTEIN, Helen NILSSON, Helen JOHANSSON (41' Pärnilla LARSSON), Anneli ANDELEN, Lena VIDEKULL.   (Coach: Not known).

Referee: Léon SCHELINGS (BEL)   Attendance: 609.

Goals: 30' Lena VIDEKULL 0-1, 33' Janne RASMUSSEN 1-1.

Yellow Card: Lotte BAGGE.

07.11.1992   Millmoor, Rotherham: England – Italy 0-3 (0-0).

ENGLAND: Tracey DAVIDSON, Louise WALLER, Clare TAYLOR, Sue LAW, Marie-Anne SPACEY, Janice MURRAY, Kerry DAVIS, Gillian COULTARD, Deborah BAMPTON, Gail BORMAN, Karen WALKER. (Coach: Not known).

ITALY: Stafania ANTONINI, Raffaela SALMASO, Dolores PRESTFILLIPPO, Emma IOZZELLI, Marina CORDENONS, Elisabetta BAVAGNOLI, Adele MARSILETTI, Silvia FIORINI, Federica D'ASTOLFO, Antonella CARTA, Carolina MORACE. (Coach: Sergio GUENZA).

Referee: José MENDES PRATA (POR)   Attendance: Not known.

Goals: 53' Adele MARSILETTI 0-1, 55', 78' Carolina MORACE 0-2, 0-3.

Yellow Card: Federica D'ASTOLFO (ITA).

14.11.1992   Jahnstadion, Rheine: Germany – Russia 0-0.

GERMANY: Manuela GOLLER, Britta UNSLEBER, Manuela SCHULTEALBERT (41' Birgitt AUSTERMÜHL), Jutta NARDENBACH, Doris FITSCHEN, Bettina WIEGMANN, Martina VOSS-TECKLENBURG, Katja BORNSCHEIN (56' Michaela KUBAT), Heidi MOHR, Silvia NEID, Maren MEINERT. (Coach: Gero BISANZ).

RUSSIA: Svetlana PETKO, Marina BURAKOVA, Natalia BUNDUKI, Elena KONONOVA, Ludmilla KOROBITSYNA, KONIAKOVA, Irina GRIGORIEVA, Natalia EMELIANOVA, KOUTCHER, Galina DOBICHINA, Elena SOTNIKOVA. (Coach: Not known).

Referee: Frank McDONALD (NIR)   Attendance: 2,431.

Yellow Card: Natalia EMELIANOVA (RUS).

SEMI-FINALS

29.06.1993   Sportilla, Santa Sofia: Norway – Denmark 1-0 (0-0).

NORWAY: Reidun SETH, Katrine NYSVEEN, Nina NYMARK JAKOBSEN, Anne NYMARK RYLANDSHOLM, Heidi STØRE, Gro ESPESETH, Agnete CARLSEN, Ann-Kristin AARONES (46' Kristin SANDBERG), Cathrine ZABOROWSKI, Linda MEDALEN, Birthe HEGSTAD (38' Hege RIISE). (Coach: Even PELLERUD).

DENMARK: Helle BJERREGAARD, Karina SEFRON, Bonny MADSEN, Irene STELLING, Susan MACKENSIE, Marianne JENSEN (61' Lisbet KOLDING), Rikke HOLM, Lotte BAGGE (67' Janne RASMUSSEN), Annette TYCHOSEN, Hanne NISSEN, Helle JENSEN. (Coach: Keld GANTZHORN).

Referee: Plarent KOTHERJA (ALB)   Attendance: 1,000.

Goal: 63' Anne NYMARK RYLANDSHOLM 1-0.

Yellow Card: Karina SEFRON (DEN).

30.06.1993   Romeo Neri, Rimini: Italy – Germany 1-1 (0-0, 1-1, 1-1).

ITALY: Giorgia BRENZAN, Raffaela SALMASO, Emma IOZZELLI, Marina CORDENONS, Elisabetta BAVAGNOLI (100' Rita GUARINO), Adele MARSILETTI, Maria MARIOTTI, Silvia FIORINI (57' Bianca BALDELLI), Feriana FERRAGUZZI, Rosa CIARDI, Carolina MORACE. (Coach: Sergio GUENZA).

GERMANY: Manuela GOLLER, Dagmar POHLMANN, Jutta NARDENBACH, Birgitt AUSTERMÜHL, Anouschka BERNHARD, Doris FITSCHEN, Bettina WIEGMANN, Heidi MOHR, Katja BORNSCHEIN (100' Britta UNSLEBER), Silvia NEID, Maren MEINERT. (Coach: Gero BISANZ).

Referee: Anders FRISK (SWE)   Attendance: 3,000.

Goals: 56' Heidi MOHR 0-1, 63' Carolina MORACE 1-1.

Yellow Cards: Maria MARIOTTI, Silvia FIORINI (ITA), Silvia NEID (GER).

Red card: Jutta NARDENBACH (GER).

Italy won 4-3 on penalties following extra time.

Penalties: Bettina WIEGMANN 0-1, Adele MARSILETTI 1-1, Birgitt AUSTERMÜHL 1-2, Raffaela SALMASO 2-2, Dagmar POHLMANN 2-3, Feriana FERRAGUZZI 3-3, Unknown German player missed, Emma IOZZELLI 4-3.

3RD PLACE MATCH

03.07.1993   Stadio Comunale, Cesenatico: Denmark – Germany 3-1 (3-1).

DENMARK: Helle BJERREGAARD, Karina SEFRON, Bonny MADSEN, Lisbet KOLDING, Rikke HOLM, Lotte BAGGE, Irene STELLING, Susan MACKENSIE, Helle JENSEN (67' Marianne JENSEN), Annette TYCHOSEN (55' Janne RASMUSSEN), Hanne NISSEN. (Coach: Keld GANTZHORN).

GERMANY: Silke ROTTENBERG, Birgitt AUSTERMÜHL, Dagmar POHLMANN (41' Britta UNSLEBER), Jutta NARDENBACH, Anouschka BERNHARD, Doris FITSCHEN, Bettina WIEGMANN, Heidi MOHR, Katja BORNSCHEIN (60' Steffio JONES), Silvia NEID, Maren MEINERT. (Coach: Gero BISANZ).

Referee: Dick JOL (HOL)   Attendance: 500.

Goals: 11' Susan MACKENSIE 1-0, 31' Maren MEINERT 1-1, 36' Hanne NISSEN 2-1, 42' Susan MACKENSIE 3-1.

Yellow Cards: Rikke HOLM.

FINAL

04.07.1993   Dino Manuzzi, Cesena: Norway – Italy 1-0 (0-0).

NORWAY: Reidun SETH, Katrine NYSVEEN, Nina NYMARK JAKOBSEN, Anne NYMARK RYLANDSHOLM, Cathrine ZABOROWSKI, Hege RIISE, Heidi STØRE, Gro ESPESETH, Agnete CARLSEN, Ann-Kristin AARONES (41' Birthe HEGSTAD), Linda MEDALEN (79' Kristin SANDBERG).   (Coach: Even PELLERUD).

ITALY: Giorgia BRENZAN, Raffaela SALMASO (55' Dolores PRESTFILIPPO), Emma IOZZELLI, Marina CORDENONS, Elisabetta BAVAGNOLI, Adele MARSILETTI, Maria MARIOTTI, Feriana FERRAGUZZI, Federica D'ASTOLFO, Rosa CIARDI (75' Rita GUARINO), Carolina MORACE. (Coach: Sergio GUENZA).

Referee: Alfred WIESER (AUT)   Attendance: 7,000.

Goals: 75' Birthe HEGSTAD 1-0.

Yellow Cards: Birthe HEGSTAD, Raffaela SALMASO, Federica D'ASTOLFO.

Norway were European Champions

UEFA EUROPEAN WOMEN'S CHAMPIONSHIP
EURO 1995

(The quarter-finals and semi-finals were played on a home and away basis)

QUARTER-FINALS

08.10.1994 Laugardsvöllur, Reykjavik: Iceland – England 1-2 (1-1).

ICELAND: Sigridur Fanney PÁLSDÓTTIR, Audur SKÚLADÓTTIR, Halldóra Vanda SIGURGEIRSDÓTTIR, Gudrún SAEMUNDSDÓTTIR, Sigrún OTTARSDÓTTIR (69' Gudrún Jóna KRISTJÁNSDÓTTIR), Margrét OLAFSDÓTTIR, Gudlaug JÓNSDÓTTIR, Asthildur HELGADÓTTIR, Asta GUNNLAUGSDÓTTIR, Andrea Olga FAERSETH, Ragna Lóa STEFÁNSDÓTTIR. (Coach: Logi ÓLAFSSON).

ENGLAND: Lesley HIGGS, Clare TAYLOR, Donna SMITH, Kirsty PEALLING, Deborah BAMPTON, Sian WILLIAMS, Marie Anne SPACEY, Janice MURRAY, Kerry DAVIS, Gilian COULTARD, Karen WALKER. (Coach: Ted COPELAND).

Referee: Timo KELTANEN (FIN)   Attendance: 600.

Goals: 5' Gilian COULTARD 0-1, 31' Margrét OLAFSDÓTTIR 1-1, 61' Kerry DAVIS 1-2.

Yellow Card: Kirsty PEALLING.

09.10.1994 Stroitel, Selyatino: Russia – Germany 0-1 (0-0).

RUSSIA: Svetlana PETKO, Valentina BARKOVA, Ludmilla KOROBITSYNA, Elena KONONOVA, Marina BURAKOVA, Aleksandra SVETLITSKAYA, Natalia KOPKOVA, Irina GRIGORIEVA, Tatiana EGOROVA, Nadezhda BOSIKOVA, Larissa SAVINA. (Coach: Not known).

GERMANY: Manuela GOLLER, Birgitt AUSTERMÜHL, Anoushka BERNHARD, Bettina WIEGMANN, Martino VOSS-TECKLENBURG, Doris FITSCHEN, Katja BORNSCHEIN (33' Pia WUNDERLICH), Heidi MOHR, Patricia BROCKER, Silvia NEID, Maren MEINERT (63' Birgit PRINZ).   (Coach: Gero BISANZ).

Referee: Luben ANGELOV (BUL)   Attendance: 1,200.

Goal: 70' Heidi MOHR (p) 0-1.

Yellow Card: Ludmilla KOROBITSYNA.

15.10.1994   Hjørring Stadion, Hjørring: Denmark – Sweden 2-0 (0-0).

DENMARK: Dorthe LARSEN, Karina SEFRON, Bonny MADSEN, Birgit CHRISTENSEN, Lotte BAGGE, Irene STELLING, Lisbet KOLDING, Katrine SØNDERGAARD PEDERSEN, Helle JENSEN, Annette TYCHOSEN (77' Anne NIELSEN), Lena MADSEN (56' Gitte KROGH). (Coach: Keld GANTZHORN).

SWEDEN: Elisabeth LEIDINGE, Kristin BENGTSSON, Eva ZEIKFALVY, Annika NESSVOLD, Malin LUNDGREN, Asa JAKOBSSON, Malin ANDERSSON (65' Ulrika KALTE), Sofia JOHANSSON (83' Helen NILSSON), Anneli ANDELEN, Lena VIDEKULL, Helen JOHANSSON. (Coach: Bengt SIMONSON).

Referee: Fernand MEESE (BEL)   Attendance: 770.

Goals: 84' Anne NIELSEN 1-0, 87' Gitte KROGH 2-0.

15.10.1994   Danilo Martelli, Mantova: Italy – Norway 1-3 (1-2).

ITALY: Stefania ANTONINI, Raffaela SALMASO, Emma IOZZELLI, Marina CORDENONS, Elisabetta BAVAGNOLI, Silvia FIORINI (57' Rita GUARINO), Federica D'ASTOLFO, Bianca BALDELLI, BICHI (31' PITTALIS), Manuela TESSE, Carolina MORACE. (Coach: Not known).

NORWAY: Reidun SETH, Nina NYMARK JAKOBSEN, Anne NYMARK RYLANDSHOLM, Merete MYKLEBUST, Heidi STØRE, Gro ESPESETH, Agnete CARLSEN, Ann-Kristin AARONES, Hege RIISE, Linda MEDALEN, Kristin SANDBERG. (Coach: Even PELLERUD).

Referee: Mateo BEUSAN (CRO)   Attendance: 3,050.

Goals: 10' Linda MEDALEN 0-1, 14' Raffaela SALMASO 1-1, 28' Anne NYMARK RYLANDSHOLM 1-2 (p), 86' Kristin SANDBERG 1-3.

Yellow Cards: Stefania ANTONINI, Bianca BALDELLI, Agnete CARLSEN, Linda MEDALEN.

27.10.1994   Stadion an der Bremer Brücke, Osnabrück: Germany – Russia 4-0 (4-0).

GERMANY: Manuela GOLLER (46' Elke WALTHER), Sandra MINNERT, Birgitt AUSTERMÜHL, Pia WUNDERLICH (54' Katja BORNSCHEIN), Bettina WIEGMANN, Martino VOSS-TECKLENBURG, Doris FITSCHEN, Heidi MOHR (75' Birgit PRINZ), Patricia BROCKER, Silvia NEID, Maren MEINERT. (Coach: Gero BISANZ).

RUSSIA: Svetlana PETKO, Ludmilla KOROBITSYNA, Elena KONONOVA, Marina BURAKOVA, Natalia BUNDUKI, LITVINOVA, Aleksandra SVETLITSKAYA, Natalia KOPKOVA, Irina GRIGORIEVA, Tatiana EGOROVA, Larissa SAVINA.
(Coach: Not known).

Referee: Gheorghe CONSTANTIN (ROM)   Attendance: 4,600.

Goals: 5' Heidi MOHR 1-0, 23' Patricia BROCKER 2-0, 29' Silvia NEID 3-0, 45' Heidi MOHR 4-0.

Yellow Card: Maren MEINERT.

29.10.1994   Malmö Stadion, Malmö: Sweden – Denmark 3-0 (3-0).

SWEDEN: Elisabeth LEIDINGE, Kristin BENGTSSON, Eva ZEIKFALVY, Annika NESSVOLD, Asa JAKOBSSON, Malin ANDERSSON, Ulrika KALTE (30' Sofia JOHANSSON), Helen JOHANSSON, Anneli ANDELEN, Lena VIDEKULL, Pia SUNDHAGE (54' Malin LUNDGREN). (Coach: Bengt SIMONSON).

DENMARK: Dorthe LARSEN, Karina SEFRON, Bonny MADSEN, Birgit CHRISTENSEN, Irene STELLING, Lisbet KOLDING, Katrine SØNDERGAARD PEDERSEN, Helle JENSEN, Annette TYCHOSEN (61' Gitte KROGH), Anne NIELSEN, Lena MADSEN (46' Marianne JENSEN). (Coach: Keld GANTZHORN).

Referee: István VADA (HUN)   Attendance: 958.

Goals: 8' Anneli ANDELEN 1-0, 31' Sofia JOHANSSON 2-0, 45' Anneli ANDELEN 3-0.

29.10.1994   Bislett, Oslo: Norway – Italy 4-2 (2-1).

NORWAY: Reidun SETH, Nina NYMARK JAKOBSEN, Anne NYMARK RYLANDSHOLM, Merete MYKLEBUST, Heidi STØRE, Gro ESPESETH, Agnete CARLSEN, Ann-Kristin AARONES (72' Marianne PETTERSEN), Hege RIISE, Linda MEDALEN (80' Randi LEINAN), Kristin SANDBERG. (Coach: Even PELLERUD).

ITALY: Stefania ANTONINI, Dolores PRESTFILIPPO, Emma IOZZELLI, Marina CORDENONS, Monica CAPRINI (46' Monia GAZZAROLI), Tatiana ZORRI, Manuela TESSA, PITTALIS, Antonella CARTA, Rita GUARINO, Carolina MORACE.
(Coach: Not known).

Referee: Herbert BARR (NIR)   Attendance: 4,122.

Goals: 1' Kristin SANDBERG 1-0, 30' Anne NYMARK RYLANDSHOLM 2-0 (p), 34' Carolina MORACE 2-1, 65' Anne NYMARK RYLANDSHOLM 3-1, 84' Marianne PETTERSEN 4-1, 87' Rita GUARINO 4-2.

Yellow Cards: Gro ESPESETH, Dolores PRESTFILIPPO, Tatiana ZORRI.

30.10.1994   Withdean Stadium, Brighton: England – Iceland 2-1 (1-1).

ENGLAND: Lesley HIGGS, Clare TAYLOR, Donna SMITH, Kirsty PEALLING, Deborah BAMPTON, Sian WILLIAMS, Marie Anne SPACEY, Janice MURRAY, Kerry DAVIS (46' Louise WALLER), Gilian COULTARD, Karen WALKER.   (Coach: Ted COPELAND).

ICELAND: Sigridur Fanney PÁLSDÓTTIR, Audur SKÚLADÓTTIR (37' Helga HANNESDÓTTIR), Halldóra Vanda SIGURGEIRSDÓTTIR, Gudrún SAEMUNDSDÓTTIR, Gudrún Jóna KRISTJÁNSDÓTTIR, Margrét OLAFSDÓTTIR, Gudlaug JÓNSDÓTTIR, Asthildur HELGADÓTTIR, Asta GUNNLAUGSDÓTTIR, Andrea Olga FAERSETH (78' Kristin Anna ARNPÓRSDÓTTIR), Ragna Lóa STEFÁNSDÓTTIR.
(Coach: Logi ÓLAFSSON).

Referee: Richard O'HANLON (IRL)   Attendance: 2,000.

Goals: 13' Gilian COULTARD 1-0, 36' Asta GUNNLAUGSDÓTTIR 1-1, 65' Marie Anne SPACEY 2-1.

Yellow Cards: Louise WALLER, Gudrún SAEMUNDSDÓTTIR.

SEMI-FINALS

12.11.1994   Vicarage Road, Watford: England – Germany 1-4 (1-1).

ENGLAND: Lesley HIGGS, Clare TAYLOR, Kirsty PEALLING, Samantha BRITTON, Janice MURRAY, Kerry DAVIS, Gilian COULTARD, Karen WALKER, Karen BURKE, Deborah BAMPTON, Karen FARLEY.   (Coach: Ted COPELAND).

GERMANY: Manuela GOLLER, Sandra MINNERT (46' Pia WUNDERLICH), Birgitt AUSTERMÜHL, Anouschka BERNHARD, Bettina WIEGMANN, Martino VOSS-TECKLENBURG, Doris FITSCHEN, Heidi MOHR, Patricia BROCKER (68' Birgit PRINZ), Silvia NEID, Maren MEINERT.   (Coach: Gero BISANZ).

Referee: Sándor PILLER (HUN)   Attendance: 800.

Goals: 7' Karen FARLEY 1-0, 32' Heidi MOHR 1-1, 68' Patricia BROCKER 1-2, 80' Heidi MOHR 1-3, 87' Bettina WIEGMANN 1-4 (p).

26.02.1995   Kristiansand Stadion, Kristiansand: Norway – Sweden 4-3 (1-1).

NORWAY: Reidun SETH, Nina NYMARK JAKOBSEN (60' Monica ENLID), Merete MYKLEBUST, Anita WAAGE, Heidi STØRE, Gro ESPESETH, Anne NYMARK RYLANDSHOLM, Ann-Kristin AARONES, Hege RIISE, Linda MEDALEN, Kristin SANDBERG.   (Coach: Even PELLERUD).

SWEDEN: Elisabeth LEIDINGE, Kristin BENGTSSON, Eva ZEIKFALVY, Annika NESSVOLD, Asa JAKOBSSON, Malin ANDERSSON, Ulrika KALTE, Helen JOHANSSON, Anneli ANDELEN, Lena VIDEKULL, Pia SUNDHAGE.   (Coach: Bengt SIMONSON).

Referee: Finn LAMBEK (DEN)   Attendance: 2,098.

Goals: 15' Ulrike KALTE 0-1, 44' Ann-Kristin AARONES 1-1, 55' Anneli ANDELEN 1-2, 60' Kristin SANDBERG 2-2, 61' Helen JOHANSSON 2-3, 64' Ann-Kristin AARONES 3-3, 89' Anita WAAGE 4-3.'

Yellow Card: Helen JOHANSSON.

28.02.1995   Ruhrstadion, Bochum: Germany – England 2-1 (1-1).

GERMANY: Manuela GOLLER, Dagmar POHLMANN (80' Ursula LOHN), Jutta NARDENBACH, Birgitt AUSTERMÜHL, Anouschka BERNHARD, Bettina WIEGMANN, Martino VOSS-TECKLENBURG, Heidi MOHR, Patricia BROCKER (46' Birgit PRINZ), Silvia NEID, Maren MEINERT.   (Coach: Gero BISANZ).

ENGLAND: Pauline COPE, Louise WALLER, Clare TAYLOR, Tina MAPES, Sian WILLIAMS, Marie Anne SPACEY, Kerry DAVIS, Gilian COULTARD, Karen WALKER, Karen BURKE, Karen FARLEY.   (Coach: Ted COPELAND).

Referee: Kostadin GERGINOV (BUL)   Attendance: 7,000.

Goals: 1' Karen FARLEY 0-1, 34' Louise WALLER 1-1 (og), 79' Birgit PRINZ 2-1.

05.03.1995   Stadsparksvallen, Jönköping: Sweden – Norway 4-1 (0-1).

SWEDEN: Elisabeth LEIDINGE, Kristin BENGTSSON, Eva ZEIKFALVY, Annika NESSVOLD, Anneli OLSSON, Malin ANDERSSON, Anneli ANDELEN, Ulrika KALTE (78' Susanne HEDBERG), Helen JOHANSSON (46' Lena VIDEKULL), Pia SUNDHAGE.   (Coach: Bengt SIMONSON).

NORWAY: Reidun SETH, Nina NYMARK JAKOBSEN (65' Marianne PETTERSEN), Anita WAAGE, Anne NYMARK RYLANDSHOLM, Merete MYKLEBUST, Ann-Kristin AARONES, Hege RIISE, Gro ESPESETH, Kristin SANDBERG (55' Randi LEINAN), Linda MEDALEN, Birthe HEGSTAD.   (Coach: Even PELLERUD).

Referee: Willie YOUNG (SCO)   Attendance: 2,147.

Goals: 28' Linda MEDALEN 0-1, 53' Ulrika KALTE 1-1, 59', 61', 76' Lena VIDEKULL 2-1, 3-1, 4-1.

FINAL

26.03.1995 Fritz-Walter-Stadion, Kaiserslautern: Germany – Sweden 3-2 (1-1).

GERMANY: Manuela GOLLER, Dagmar POHLMANN, Birgitt AUSTERMÜHL, Anouschka BERNHARD, Bettina WIEGMANN, Martino VOSS-TECKLENBURG (90' Pia WUNDERLICH), Heidi MOHR, Ursula LOHN, Patricia BROCKER (62' Birgit PRINZ), Silvia NEID, Maren MEINERT. (Coach: Gero BISANZ).

SWEDEN: Elisabeth LEIDINGE, Kristin BENGTSSON, Eva ZEIKFALVY (78' Malin LUNDGREN), Annika NESSVOLD, Asa JAKOBSSON, Anneli OLSSON (59' Sofia JOHANSSON), Malin ANDERSSON, Anneli ANDELEN, Ulrika KALTE, Lena VIDEKULL, Pia SUNDHAGE. (Coach: Bengt SIMONSON).

Referee: Ilkka KOHO (FIN)   Attendance: 8,500.

Goals: 6' Malin ANDERSSON 0-1, 33' Maren MEINERT 1-1, 64' Birgit PRINZ 2-1, 85' Bettina WIEGMANN 3-1, 89' Anneli ANDELEN 3-2.

Dagmar Pohlmann missed a penalty in the 8th minute.

Germany were European Champions

UEFA EUROPEAN WOMEN'S CHAMPIONSHIP
EURO 1997

For the first time there were group phases A and B. The number 1 and 2 of the group proceed through the semi-finals and the winners through to the final. All matches were played in Norway and Sweden.

GROUP A

29.06.1997   Nobelstadion, Karlskoga: France – Spain 1-1 (0-1).

FRANCE: Sandrine ROUX, Cécile LOCATELLI, Helene HILLION-GUILLEMIN, Jocelyne GOUT (77' Candie HERBERT), Corinne DIACRE, Élodie WOOCK (64' Stéphanie TROGNON), Sandrine SOUBEYRAND, Anne ZÉNONI, Angélique ROUJAS, Marinette PICHON, Stepanie MUGNERET-BEGHE. (Coach: Elisabeth LOISEL).

SPAIN: Maria ROSER, Judith COROMINAS, Maria ARÁNTZAZU, TONA, Marina NOHALEZ, Rosa CASTILLO, Beatriz BERNARDOS, Maria LUISA PUNAL, Yolanda MATEOS, Mar PRIETO, Alicia FUENTES (10' Isabel PAREJO). (Coach: Ignacio QUEREDA).

Referee: Gitte NIELSEN (DEN)   Attendance: 920.

Goals: 14' Isabel PAREJO 0-1, 52' Angélique ROUJAS 1-1.

Yellow Card: TONA.

29.06.1997   Tingvalla IP, Karlstad: Sweden – Russia 2-1 (0-0).

SWEDEN: Ulrika KARLSSON, Karolina WESTBERG, Jane TÖRNQVIST, Asa LONNQVIST, Kristin BENGTSSON, Malin SWEDBERG, Anna POHJANEN, Carina JERLOV (46' Malin ALLBERG), Malin ANDERSSON (46' Camilla NEPTUNE), Victoria SVENSSON, Hanna LJUNGBERG (46' Eva ZEIKFALVY). (Coach: Marika DOMANSKI-LYFORS).

RUSSIA: Svetlana PETKO, Elena KONONOVA (46' Natalia BARBASHINA), Marina BURAKOVA, Valentina BARKOVA (46' Aleksandra SVETLITSKAYA), Tatiana TCHEVERDA, Galina KOMAROVA, Irina GRIGORIEVA, Alena DMITRENKO, Elena DENCHTCHIK, Larissa SAVINA, Martina DIKAREVA (46' Tatiana EGOROVA). (Coach: Yuriy BYSTRITSKIY).

Referee: Christine FRAI (GER)   Attendance: 3,829.

Goals: 88' Larissa SAVINA 0-1, 89' Hanna LJUNGBERG 1-1, 90' Anna POHJANEN 2-1.

Yellow Cards: Marina BURAKOVA, Tatiana TCHEVERDA, Galina KOMAROVA.

02.07.1997   Nobelstadion, Karlskoga: Spain – Sweden 0-1 (0-1).

SPAIN: Maria ROSER, Judith COROMINAS, Maria ARÁNTZAZU, TONA, Marina NOHALEZ, Rosa CASTILLO, Beatriz BERNARDOS, Yolanda MATEOS (46' Maria LUISA PUNAL), MAIDER, Angeles PAREJO, Mar PRIETO. (Coach: Ignacio QUEREDA).

SWEDEN: Annelie NILSSON, Karolina WESTBERG, Jane TÖRNQVIST, Asa LONNQVIST, Kristin BENGTSSON, Malin SWEDBERG, Anna POHJANEN, Malin ALLBERG (46' Kristin JONSSON), Malin ANDERSSON, Victoria SVENSSON (46' Cristin LILJA), Hanna LJUNGBERG (46' Eva ZEIKFALVY).
(Coach: Marika DOMANSKI-LYFORS).

Referee: Vibeke KARLSEN (NOR)   Attendance: 3,403.

Goal: 7' Judith COROMINAS 0-1 (og).

Yellow Cards: TONA, Judith COROMINAS, Jane TÖRNQVIST.

02.07.1997   Tingvalla IP, Karlstad: Russia – France 1-3 (0-1).

RUSSIA: Svetlana PETKO, Elena KONONOVA, Tatiana TCHEVERDA, Marina BURAKOVA, Aleksandra SVETLITSKAYA, Galina KOMAROVA, Irina GRIGORIEVA, Alena DMITRENKO, Tatiana EGOROVA, Elena DENCHTCHIK, Larissa SAVINA.
(Coach: Yuriy BYSTRITSKIY).

FRANCE: Sandrine ROUX, Cécile LOCATELLI, Helene HILLION-GUILLEMIN, Corinne DIACRE, Élodie WOOCK, Stéphanie TROGNON, Sandrine SOUBEYRAND, Anne ZÉNONI (32' Candie HERBERT), Angélique ROUJAS (82' Emmanuelle SYKORA), Marinette PICHON (90' Sandrine RINGLER), Stepanie MUGNERET-BEGHE.
(Coach: Elisabeth LOISEL).

Referee: Cristina GOZZI (ITA)   Attendance: 626.

Goals: 26' Angélique ROUJAS 0-1, 52' Irina GRIGORIEVA 1-1, 57', 74' Angélique ROUJAS 1-2, 1-3.

Yellow Card: Elena KONONOVA.

05.07.1997   Tingvalla IP, Karlstad: Sweden – France 3-0 (3-0).

SWEDEN: Ulrika KARLSSON, Eva ZEIKFALVY, Karolina WESTBERG, Jane TÖRNQVIST, Asa LONNQVIST, Kristin BENGTSSON (46' Anneli WAHLGREN), Malin SWEDBERG, Anna POHJANEN, Malin ANDERSSON, Victoria SVENSSON (46' Malin ALLBERG), Hanna LJUNGBERG (45' Kristin JONSSON).
(Coach: Marika DOMANSKI-LYFORS).

FRANCE: Sandrine ROUX, Cécile LOCATELLI, Helene HILLION-GUILLEMIN, Corinne DIACRE, Élodie WOOCK, Stéphanie TROGNON (75' Aude BANASIAK), Sandrine SOUBEYRAND, Angélique ROUJAS, Marinette PICHON (46' Anne ZÉNONI), Candie HERBERT (46' Emmanuelle SYKORA), Stepanie MUGNERET-BEGHE.
(Coach: Elisabeth LOISEL).

Referee: Vibeke KARLSEN (NOR)   Attendance: 2,757.

Goals: 17' Malin ANDERSSON 1-0 (p), 21' Cécile LOCATELLI 2-0 (og), 45' Kristin JONSSON 3-0.

Yellow Cards: Élodie WOOCK, Sandrine SOUBEYRAND.

05.07.1997   Nobelstadion, Karlskoga: Russia – Spain 0-1 (0-0).

RUSSIA: Svetlana PETKO, Elena KONONOVA (46' Martina DIKAREVA), Tatiana TCHEVERDA, Marina BURAKOVA, Aleksandra SVETLITSKAYA, Galina KOMAROVA, Irina GRIGORIEVA, Alena DMITRENKO, Tatiana EGOROVA, Elena DENCHTCHIK, Larissa SAVINA. (Coach: Yuriy BYSTRITSKIY).

SPAIN: Maria ROSER, Judith COROMINAS, Maria ARÁNTZAZU, TONA, Marina NOHALEZ, Rosa CASTILLO, Beatriz BERNARDOS, Yolanda MATEOS, Maria Luisa PUNAL, Alicia FUENTES (46' Isabel PAREJO), Mar Prieto.   (Coach: Ignacio QUEREDA).

Referee: Regina BELKSMA-KONINK (HOL)   Attendance: Not known.

Yellow Cards: Marina BURAKOVA, Martina DIKAREVA.

FINAL STANDINGS

1.	SWEDEN	3	3	0	0	6	-	1	9
2.	SPAIN	3	1	1	1	2	-	2	4
3.	FRANCE	3	1	1	1	4	-	5	4
4.	RUSSIA	3	0	0	3	2	-	6	0

GROUP B

30.06.1997 Melløs Stadion, Moss: Germany – Italy 1-1 (0-0).

GERMANY: Silke ROTTENBERG, Sandra MINNERT, Pia WUNDERLICH, Bettina WIEGMANN, Martina VOSS-TECKLENBURG (75' Claudia MÜLLER), Kerstin STEGEMANN, Steffi JONES, Doris FITSCHEN, Sandra SMISEK, Birgit PRINZ, Maren MEINERT. (Coach: Tina THEUNE).

ITALY: Giorgia BRENZAN, Daniela TAVALAZZI, Raffaela SALMASO, Marinella PIOLANTNI (69' Simona NANNINI), Emma IOZZELLI, Damiana DE LANA, Federica D'ASTOLFO, Rosa CIARDI, Antonella CARTA, Patrizia PANICO (42' Rita GUARINO), Carolina MORACE. (Coach: Sergio GUENZA).

Referee: Katriina ELOVIRTA (FIN) Attendance: 713.

Goals: 49' Maren MEINERT 1-0, 71' Antonella CARTA 1-1.

Yellow Cards: Sandra MINNERT, Maren MEINERT.

Red card: 55' Federica D'ASTOLFO.

30.06.1997 Åråsen Stadion, Lillestrøm: Denmark – Norway 0-5 (0-2).

DENMARK: Dorthe LARSEN, Kamma FLAENG, Karina SEFRON, Bonny MADSEN, Rikke HOLM, Jeanne AXELSEN, Anne NIELSEN, Janni JOHANSEN (69' Gitte KROGH), Lene TERP, Merete PEDERSEN (90' Irene STELLING), Marlene KRISTENSEN (57' Chrstina PETERSEN). (Coach: Jørgen HVIDEMOSE).

NORWAY: Bente NORDBY, Heidi STØRE (76' Merete MYKLEBUST), Anne NYMARK RYLANDSHOLM, Gøril KRINGEN (62' Henriette VIKER), Hege RIISE, Unni LEHN (71' Margunn HUMLESTØL), Gro ESPESETH, Agnete CARLSEN, Ann-Kristin AARONES, Marianne PETTERSEN, Linda MEDALEN. (Coach: Per-Mathias HØGMO).

Referee: Regina BELKSMA-KONINK (HOL) Attendance: 4,221.

Goals: 16', 18', 50' Marianne PETTERSEN 0-1, 0-2, 0-3, 56' Heidi STØRE 0-4, 80' Marianne PETTERSEN 0-5.

03.07.1997   Åråsen Stadion, Lillestrøm: Italy – Denmark 2-2 (1-1).

ITALY: Giorgia BRENZAN, Daniela TAVALAZZI, Raffaela SALMASO, Emma IOZZELLI, Simona NANNINI (48' Cristina MURELLI), Silvia FIORINI, Rosa CIARDI, Antonella CARTA, Manuele TESSE, Rita GUARINO (43' Roberta ULIVI / 65' Patrizia PANICO), Carolina MORACE. (Coach: Sergio GUENZA).

DENMARK: Dorthe LARSEN, Kamma FLAENG (85' Katrine SØNDERGAARD PEDERSEN), Bonny MADSEN, Rikke HOLM, Jeanne AXELSEN, Anne NIELSEN, Hanne SAND, Janni JOHANSEN, Lene TERP, Merete PEDERSEN, Gitte KROGH (55' Louise HANSEN). (Coach: Jørgen HVIDEMOSE).

Referee: Eva OEDLUND (SWE)   Attendance: 538.

Goals: 22' Lene TERP 0-1, 45' Carolina MORACE 1-1, 61' Merete PEDERSEN 1-2, 73' Carolina MORACAE 2-2.

03.07.1997   Melløs Stadion, Moss: Norway – Germany 0-0.

NORWAY: Bente NORDBY, Heidi STØRE, Anne NYMARK RYLANDSHOLM, Gøril KRINGEN (51' Henriette VIKER), Hege RIISE (83' Monica KNUDSEN), Unni LEHN (66' Margunn HUMLESTØL), Gro ESPESETH, Agnete CARLSEN, Ann-Kristin AARONES, Marianne PETTERSEN, Linda MEDALEN. (Coach: Per-Mathias HØGMO).

GERMANY: Silke ROTTENBERG, Sandra MINNERT, Pia WUNDERLICH, Bettina WIEGMANN, Martina VOSS-TECKLENBURG (41' Monika MEYER), Kerstin STEGEMANN, Steffi JONES, Doris FITSCHEN, Sandra SMISEK (49' Inken BECHER), Birgit PRINZ, Maren MEINERT. (Coach: Tina THEUNE).

Referee: Nicole PETIGNAT (SUI)   Attendance: 7,666.

06.07.1997   Melløs Stadion, Moss: Denmark – Germany 0-2 (0-0).

DENMARK: Dorthe LARSEN, Kamma FLAENG, Rikke HOLM, Jeanne AXELSEN (69' Katrine SØNDERGAARD PEDERSEN), Anne NIELSEN, Louise HANSEN, Irene STELLING (90' Christina PEDERSEN), Janni JOHANSEN, Lene TERP, Hanne SAND (22' Gitte KROGH), Merete PEDERSEN. (Coach: Jørgen HVIDEMOSE).

GERMANY: Silke ROTTENBERG, Sonja FUSS, Inken BECHER, Melanie HOFFMANN (46' Monika MEYER), Pia WUNDERLICH, Steffi JONES, Doris FITSCHEN, Bettina WIEGMANN, Kerstin STEGEMANN, Sandra SMISEK (46' Ariane HINGST), Birgit PRINZ. (Coach: Tina THEUNE).

Referee: Katriina ELOVIRTA (FIN)   Attendance: 520.

Goals: 82' Monika MEYER 0-1, 90' Birgit PRINZ 0-2.

Yellow Cards: Inken BECHER, Birgit PRINZ, Monika MEYER.

06.07.1997   Åråsen Stadion, Lillestrøm: Norway – Italy 0-2 (0-1).

NORWAY: Bente NORDBY, Heidi STØRE (85' Margunn HUMLESTØL), Henriette VIKER (46' Anne NYMARK RYLANDSHOLM), Merete MYKLEBUST, Ann-Kristin AARONES, Hege RIISE (78' Ragnhild GULBRANDSEN), Gro ESPESETH, Agnete CARLSEN, Unni LEHN, Marianne PETTERSEN, Linda MEDALEN. (Coach: Per-Mathias HØGMO).

ITALY: Giorgia BRENZAN, Daniela TAVALAZZI, Raffaela SALMASO, Emma IOZZELLI, Damiana DE LANA (48' Simona NANNINI), Manuela TESSE, Silvia FIORINI, Federica D'ASTOLFO, Rosa CIARDI (83' Cristina MURELLI), Antonella Carta, Carolina MORACE (90' Patrizia PANICO). (Coach: Sergio GUENZA).

Referee: Eva OEDLUND (SWE)   Attendance: 4,037.

Goals: 3', 90' Carolina MORACE 0-1, 0-2.

Yellow Card: Gro ESPESETH.

FINAL STANDINGS

1.	ITALY	3	1	2	0	5	-	3	5
2.	GERMANY	3	1	2	0	3	-	1	5
3.	NORWAY	3	1	1	1	5	-	2	4
4.	DENMARK	3	0	1	2	2	-	9	1

SEMI-FINALS

09.07.1997   Tingvalla IP, Karlstad: Sweden – Germany 0-1 (0-0).

SWEDEN: Ulrika KARLSSON, Eva ZEIKFALVY (63' Cecilia SANDELL), Karolina WESTBERG, Jane TÖRNQVIST, Asa LONNQVIST, Kristin BENGTSSON, Malin SWEDBERG (86' Christin LILJA), Anna POHJANEN, Malin ANDERSSON, Victoria SVENSSON, Malin ALLBERG (46' Kristin JONSSON).
(Coach: Marika DOMANSKI-LYFORS).

GERMANY: Silke ROTTENBERG, Sandra MINNERT, Inken BECHER, Pia WUNDERLICH, Steffi JONES, Doris FITSCHEN, Bettina WIEGMANN, Kerstin STEGEMANN, Sandra SMISEK (46' Monika MEYER), Birgit PRINZ, Maren MEINERT (90' Ariane HINGST).   (Coach: Tina THEUNE).

Referee: Nicole PETIGNAT (SUI)   Attendance: 4,246.

Goal: 84' Bettina WIEGMANN 0-1.

Yellow Cards: Jane TÖRNQVIST, Inken BECHER, Birgit PRINZ, Monika MEYER.

09.07.1997   Åråsen Stadion, Lillestrøm: Italy – Spain 2-1 (2-0).

ITALY: Giorgia BRENZAN, Daniela TAVALAZZI, Emma IOZZELLI, Federica D'ASTOLFO, Rosa CIARDI, Manuela TESSE, Simona NANNINI, Cristina MURELLI, Silvia FIORINI, Patrizia PANICO (31' Rita GUARINO / 71' Damiana DE LANA), Carolina Morace. (Coach: Sergio GUENZA).

SPAIN: Maria ROSER, Judith COROMINAS, Maria ARÁNTZAZU, TONA, Marina NOHALEZ (55' Isabel PAREJO), Rosa CASTILLO (61' Nuria PÉREZ), Yolanda MATEOS (81' Mónica GONZALEZ), MAIDER, Purificación CANO, Mar PRIETO, Angeles PAREJO. (Coach: Ignacio QUEREDA).

Referee: Christina FRAI (GER   Attendance: Not known.

Goals: 11' Silvia FIORINI 1-0, 29' Carolina MORACE 2-0, 89' Angeles PAREJO 2-1.

FINAL

12.07.1997   Ullevaal Stadion, Oslo: Germany – Italy 2-0 (1-0).

GERMANY: Silke ROTTENBERG, Sandra MINNERT, Ariane HINGST, Pia WUNDERLICH, Steffi JONES, Doris FITSCHEN, Bettina WIEGMANN, Kerstin STEGEMANN, Monika MEYER (68' Claudia MÜLLER), Birgit PRINZ (81' Sandra SMISEK), Maren MEINERT (87' Claudia KLEIN).   (Coach: Tina THEUNE).

ITALY: Giorgia BRENZAN, Daniela TAVALAZZI, Raffaela SALMASO (72' Damiana DE LANA), Emma IOZZELLI, Manuela TESSE, Simona NANNINI (31' Silvia FIORINI), Federica D'ASTOLFO, Rosa CIARDI, Antonella CARTA, Patrizia PANICO (61' Rita GUARINO), Carolina MORACE.   (Coach: Sergio GUENZA).

Referee: Gitte NIELSEN (DEN)   Attendance: 2,221.

Goals: 23' Sandra MINNERT 1-0, 50' Birgit PRINZ 2-0.

Yellow Cards: Pia WUNDERLICH, Emma IOZZELLI.

Germany were European Champions

UEFA EUROPEAN WOMEN'S CHAMPIONSHIP
EURO 2001

The same format was used like EURO 1997. The number 1 and 2 of the group proceed through the semi-finals and the winners through to the final. All matches were played in Germany.

GROUP A

23.06.2001   Steigerwaldstadion, Erfurt: Germany – Sweden 3-1 (1-1).

GERMANY: Silke ROTTENBERG, Sandra MINNERT, Kerstin STEGEMANN, Steffi JONES, Doris FITSCHEN, Pia WUNDERLICH (68' Sandra SMISEK), Bettina WIEGMANN, Renate LINGOR, Maren MEINERT, Birgit PRINZ (86' Martina MÜLLER), Claudia MÜLLER (68' Ariane HINGST).   (Coach: Tina THEUNE).

SWEDEN: Caroline JÖNSSON, Karolina WESTBERG, Jane TÖRNQVIST, Hanna MARKLUND, Sara LARSSON, Malin MOSTRÖM, Tina NORDLUND, Malin ANDERSSON, Linda FAGERSTRÖM (74' Victoria SVENSSON), Elin FLYBORG (69' Therese SJÖGRAN), Hanna LJUNGBERG.   (Coach: Marika DOMANSKI-LYFORS).

Referee: Katriina ELOVIRTA (FIN)   Attendance: 10,252.

Goals: 14' Hanna LJUNGBERG 0-1, 42', 65' Claudia MÜLLER 1-1, 2-1, 78' Maren MEINERT 3-1.

Yellow Cards: Kerstin STEGEMANN, Maren MEINERT.

24.06.2001   Ernst-Abbe-Sportfeld, Jena: Russia – England 1-1 (0-1).

RUSSIA: Svetlana PETKO, Marina BURAKOVA, Elena JIKHAREVA, Natalia KARASSEVA, Galina KOMAROVA, Tatiana EGOROVA, Irina GRIGORIEVA (63' Tatiana SKOTNIKOVA), Aleksandra SVETSLITSKAYA (85' Oksana SCMACHKOVA), Elena FOMINA, Natalia BARBASHINA, Olga LETYUSHOVA (57' Olga KREMLEVA).   (Coach: Yuriy BYSTRITSKIY).

ENGLAND: Pauline COPE, Danielle MURPHY, Rachel UNITT (70' Julie FLETCHER), Becky EASTON (83' Samantha BRITTON), Mo MARLEY, Katie CHAPMAN, Karen BURKE, Tara PROCTOR, Marie Anne SPACEY, Angela BANKS (62' Kelly SMITH), Sue SMITH.   (Coach: Hope POWELL).

Referee: Rita RUIZ-TACORONTE (ESP)   Attendance: 1,253.

Goals: 45' Angela BANKS 0-1, 62' Aleksandra SVETSLITSKAYA 1-1.

Yellow Card: Natalia KARASSEVA.

27.06.2001   Steigerwaldstadion, Erfurt: Germany – Russia 5-0 (1-0).

GERMANY: Silke ROTTENBERG, Sandra MINNERT, Kerstin STEGEMANN (61' Pia WUNDERLICH), Steffi JONES, Doris FITSCHEN, Bettina WIEGMANN, Renate LINGOR (78' Navina OMILADE-KELLER), Maren MEINERT, Sandra SMISEK, Birgit PRINZ, Claudia MÜLLER (61' Ariane HINGST).   (Coach: Tina THEUNE).

RUSSIA: Svetlana PETKO, Marina BURAKOVA, Natalia FILIPPOVA, Natalia KARASSEVA (46' Ioulia ISSAEVA), Olga KARASSEVA, Galina KOMAROVA, Tatiana EGOROVA (71' Tatiana SKOTNIKOVA), Irina GRIGORIEVA, Aleksandra SVETSLITSKAYA, Elena FOMINA, Olga KREMLEVA (46' Natalia BARBASHINA). (Coach: Yuriy BYSTRITSKIY).

Referee: Bente SKOGVANG (NOR)   Attendance: 6,249.

Goals: 43' Bettina WIEGMANN 1-0, 50' Birgit PRINZ 2-0, 69' Maren MEINERT 3-0, 73', 89' Sandra SMISEK 4-0, 5-0.

Yellow Card: Olga KARASSEVA, Irina GRIGORIEVA.

27.06.2001   Ernst-Abbe-Sportfeld, Jena: Sweden – England 4-0 (2-0).

SWEDEN: Caroline JÖNSSON, Karolina WESTBERG, Jane TÖRNQVIST, Hanna MARKLUND, Kristin BENGTSSON (71' Therese SJÖGRAN), Malin MOSTRÖM, Tina NORDLUND, Malin ANDERSSON (79' Linda FAGERSTRÖM), Sofia ERIKSSON, Elin FLYBORG (53' Victoria SVENSSON), Hanna LJUNGBERG. (Coach: Marika DOMANSKI-LYFORS).

ENGLAND: Pauline COPE, Danielle MURPHY, Rachel UNITT, Becky EASTON (52' Kelly SMITH), Mo MARLEY, Samantha BRITTON, Katie CHAPMAN, Karen BURKE, Tara PROCTOR (66' Marie Anne SPACEY), Angela BANKS, Sue SMITH (46' Rachel YANKEY).   (Coach: Hope POWELL).

Referee: Claudine BROHET (BEL)   Attendance: 1,000.

Goals: 2' Jane TÖRNQVIST 1-0, 27' Kristin BENGTSSON 2-0, 74' Hanna LJUNGBERG 3-0, 82' Sofia ERIKSSON 4-0.

Yellow Cards: Marie Anne SPACEY, Kelly SMITH.

30.06.2001   Ernst-Abbe-Sportfeld, Jena: England – Germany 0-3 (0-0).

ENGLAND: Pauline COPE, Danielle MURPHY, Rachel UNITT (65' Julie FETCHER), Faye WHITE, Samantha BRITTON (75' Vicky EXLEY), Katie CHAPMAN, Karen BURKE, Tara PROCTOR, Kelly SMITH (90' Angela BANKS), Sue SMITH, Karen WALKER.
(Coach: Hope POWELL).

GERMANY: Silke ROTTENBERG, Sandra MINNERT, Steffi JONES, Doris FITSCHEN, Ariane HINGST, Pia WUNDERLICH (76' Linda BRESONIK), Bettina WIEGMANN, Renate LINGOR, Sandra SMISEK (46' Martina MÜLLER), Birgit PRINZ, Claudia MÜLLER (46' Petra WIMBERSKY). (Coach: Tina THEUNE).

Referee: Bente SKOGVANG (NOR)   Attendance: 11,312.

Goals: 57' Petra WIMBERSKY 0-1, 65' Bettina WIEGMANN 0-2, 67' Renate LINGOR 0-3.

Yellow Cards: Bettina WIEGMANN, Petra WIMBERSKY.

Kelly Smith missed a penalty in the 89th minute.

30.06.2001   Steigerwaldstadion, Erfurt: Sweden – Russia 1-0 (0-0).

SWEDEN: Caroline JÖNSSON, Karolina WESTBERG, Jane TÖRNQVIST, Hanna MARKLUND, Kristin BENGTSSON (51' Linda FAGERSTRÖM), Malin MOSTRÖM, Tina NORDLUND, Malin ANDERSSON, Sofia ERIKSSON (75' Sara LARSSON), Hanna LJUNGBERG, Victoria SVENSSON (84' Therese LUNDIN).
(Coach: Marika DOMANSKI-LYFORS).

RUSSIA: Svetlana PETKO, Marina BURAKOVA, Elena JIKHAREVA, Natalia FILIPPOVA (46' Olga KEMLEVA), Galina KOMAROVA, Tatiana EGOROVA, Irina GRIGORIEVA (65' Tatiana SKOTNIKOVA), Aleksandra SVETSLITSKAYA, Elena FOMINA (78' Oksana SHMACHKOVA), Natalia BABASHINA, Olga LETYUSHOVA.
(Coach: Yuriy BYSTRITSKIY).

Referee: Rita RUIZ-TACORONTE (ESP)   Attendance: 820.

Goal: 76' Linda FAGERSTRÖM.

Yellow Cards: Marina BURAKOVA, Galina KOMAROVA.

FINAL STANDINGS

1.	GERMANY	3	3	0	0	11	-	1	9
2.	SWEDEN	3	2	0	1	6	-	3	6
3.	RUSSIA	3	0	1	2	1	-	7	1
4.	ENGLAND	3	0	1	2	1	-	8	1

GROUP B

25.06.2001   Städtisches Waldstadion, Aalen: Italy – Denmark 2-1 (1-0).

ITALY: Giorgia BRENZAN, Daniela TAVALAZZI, Gioia MASIA (66' Anna DUO), Adele FROLLANI, Damiana DE LANA, Marina PELLIZZER, Tatiana ZORRI (82' Piera-Cassandra MAGLIO), Manuela TESSE, Federica D'ASTOLFO, Patrizia PANICO, Rita GUARINO. (Coach: Carolina MORACE).

DENMARK: Heidi JOHANSEN, Ulla KNUDSEN (33' Julie ANDERSSON), Gitte ANDERSEN, Katrine SØNDERGAARD PEDERSEN, Cathrine PAASKE SÖRENSEN (66' Julie RYDAHL), Christine BONDE, Lene TERP, Christina PETERSEN, Lene JENSEN (84' Mette JOKUMSEN), Gitte KROGH, Merete PEDERSEN. (Coach: Poul HØJMOSE).

Referee: Nicole PETIGNAT (SUI)   Attendance: 3,193.

Goals: 12', 72' Patrizia PANICO 1-0, 2-0, 74' Julie RYDAHL 2-1.

Yellow Cards: Gioia MASIA, Ulla KNUDSEN, Gitte ANDERSEN.

25.06.2001   Donaustadion, Ulm: Norway – France 3-0 (3-0).

NORWAY: Bente NORDBY, Brit SANDAUNE, Gøril KRINGEN (66' Anne BUGGE-PAULSEN), Anne TONNESSEN, Bente KVITLAND, Monica KNUDSEN (75' Unni LEHN), Hege RIISE, Solveig GULBRANDSEN, Ragnhild GULBRANDSEN, Dagny MELLGREN, Linda ORMEN (86' Anita RAPP).   (Coach: Age STEEN).

FRANCE: Corinne LAGACHE, Emmanuelle SYKORA, Corinne DIACRE, Aline RIÉRA, Sandrine SOUBEYRAND, Françoise JÉZÉQUEL (79' Gaëlle BLOUIN), Sonia BOMPASTOR, Stephanie MUGNERET-BEGHE, Anne ZÉNONI (46' Hoda LATTAF) Marinette PICHON, Angélique ROUJAS (88' Candie HERBERT).
(Coach: Elisabeth LOISEL).

Referee: Wendy THOMS (ENG)   Attendance: 3,100.

Goals: 14' Monica KNUDSEN 1-0, 18' Emmanuelle SYKORA 2-0 (og), 40' Dagny MELLGREN 3-0.

Yellow Cards: Gøril KRINGEN, Bente KVITLAND, Monica KNUDSEN.

28.06.2001   Stadion an der Kreuzeiche, Reutlingen: France – Denmark 3-4 (2-2).

FRANCE: Corinne LAGACHE, Emmanuelle SYKORA, Corinne DIACRE, Aline RIÉRA, Sandrine SOUBEYRAND, Gaëlle BLOUIN, Sonia BOMPASTOR, Stephanie MUGNERET-BEGHE (78' Candie HERBERT), Marinette PICHON (90' Marie KUBIAK), Angélique ROUJAS (78' Élodie WOOCK), Hoda LATTAF.   (Coach: Elisabeth LOISEL).

DENMARK: Heidi JOHANSEN, Gitte ANDERSEN, Julie ANDERSSON, Katrine SØNDERGAARD PEDERSEN, Cathrine PAASKE SÖRENSEN (89' Mette JOKUMSEN), Christine BONDE, Lene TERP, Christina PETERSEN, Lene JENSEN (52' Nadia KJAELDGAARD), Gitte KROGH, Merete PEDERSEN.   (Coach: Poul HØJMOSE).

Referee: Eva OEDLUND (ZWE)   Attendance: 5,400.

Goals: 15' Gitte KROGH 0-1 (p), 18' Christine BONDE 0-2, 21' Marinette PICHON 1-2, 27' Stephanie MUGNERET-BEGHE 2-2, 71' Julie ANDERSSON 2-3, 83' Gaëlle BLOUIN 3-3, 90' Gitte KROGH 3-4.

Gitte Krogh missed a penalty in the 56th minute.

28.06.2001   Stadion an der Kreuzeiche, Reutlingen: Norway – Italy 1-1 (1-1).

NORWAY: Bente NORDBY, Brit SANDAUNE, Gøril KRINGEN, Anne TONNESSEN, Bente KVITLAND, Monica KNUDSEN (69' Unni LEHN), Hege RIISE, Solveig GULBRANDSEN, Ragnhild GULBRANDSEN, Dagny MELLGREN, Linda ORMEN (46' Margunn HUMLESTØL).   (Coach: Age STEEN).

ITALY: Giorgia BRENZAN, Daniela TAVALAZZI, Gioia MASIA, Adele FROLLANI, Damiana DE LANA, Marina PELLIZZER (46' Piera-Cassandra MAGLIO), Tatiana ZORRI (82' Samantha CERONI), Manuela TESSE, Federica D'ASTOLFO, Patrizia PANICO, Rita GUARINO (66' Silvia TAGLAICARNE).   (Coach: Carolina MORACE).

Referee: Elke FIELENBACH (GER)   Attendance: 6,500.

Goals: 13' Rita GUARINO 0-1, 16' Dagny MELLGREN 1-1.

Yellow Cards: Gøril KRINGEN, Anne TONNESSEN.

01.07.2001   Städtisches Waldstadion, Aalen: Denmark – Norway 1-0 (0-0).

DENMARK: Heidi JOHANSEN, Gitte ANDERSEN, Julie ANDERSSON, Katrine SØNDERGAARD PEDERSEN, Cathrine PAASKE SÖRENSEN (78' Lise SØNDERGAARD), Nadia KJAELDGAARD (58' Lene JENSEN), Christine BONDE (87' Anja MØLLER), Lene TERP, Christina PETERSEN, Gitte KROGH, Merete PEDERSEN. (Coach: Poul HØJMOSE).

NORWAY: Bente NORDBY, Brit SANDAUNE, Anne TONNESSEN, Bente KVITLAND, Monica KNUDSEN (43' Unni LEHN), Anne BUGGE-PAULSEN, Hege RIISE, Solveig GULBRANDSEN (90' Christine BØE JENSEN), Ragnhild GULBRANDSEN, Dagny MELLGREN, Anita RAPP (71' Linda ORMEN). (Coach: Age STEEN).

Referee: Claudine BROHET (BEL)   Attendance: 3,000.

Goal: 84' Merete PEDERSEN 1-0.

01.07.2001   Donaustadion, Ulm: France – Italy 2-0 (1-0).

FRANCE: Corinne LAGACHE, Emmanuelle SYKORA, Aline RIÉRA, Élodie WOOCK, Sandrine SOUBEYRAND, Gaëlle BLOUIN, Françoise JÉZÉQUEL (77' Candie HERBERT), Severine LECOUFLE, Sonia BOMPASTOR, Stephanie MUGNERET-BEGHE, Marinette PICHON (85' Hoda LATTAF).   (Coach: Elisabeth LOISEL).

ITALY: Giorgia BRENZAN, Monica CAPRINI (39' Marina PELLIZZER), Daniela TAVALAZZI (46' Anna DUO), Gioia MASIA, Adele FROLLANI, Damiana DE LANA, Tatiana ZORRI, Manuela TESSE (90' Samantha CERONI), Federica D'ASTOLFO, Patrizia PANICO, Silvia TAGLIACARNE.   (Coach: Carolina MORACE).

Referee: Elke FIELENBACH (GER)   Attendance: 3,100.

Goals: 37' Marinette PICHON 1-0, 74' Françoise JÉZÉQUEL 2-0 (p).

Yellow Card: Stephanie MUGNERET-BEGHE.

Red card: 90' Patrizia PANICO.

FINAL STANDINGS

1.	DENMARK	3	2	0	1	6	-	5	6
2.	NORWAY	3	1	1	1	4	-	2	4
3.	ITALY	3	1	1	1	3	-	4	4
4.	FRANCE	3	1	0	2	5	-	7	3

SEMI-FINALS

04.07.2001   Donaustadion, Ulm: Germany – Norway 1-0 (0-0).

GERMANY: Silke ROTTENBERG, Sandra MINNERT (45' Ariane HINGST), Kerstin STEGEMANN, Steffi JONES, Doris FITSCHEN, Pia WUNDERLICH (57' Claudia MÜLLER), Bettina WIEGMANN, Renate LINGOR, Sandra SMISEK (70' Petra WIMBERSKY), Maren MEINERT, Birgit PRINZ. (Coach: Tina THEUNE).

NORWAY: Bente NORDBY, Brit SANDAUNE, Gøril KRINGEN, Anne TONNESSEN, Anne BUGGE-PAULSEN (44' Bente KVITLAND), Hege RIISE, Solveig GULBRANDSEN (81' Christine BØE JENSEN), Unni LEHN, Ragnhild GULBRANDSEN, Dagny MELLGREN, Linda ORMEN (68' Margunn HUMLESTØL). (Coach: Age STEEN).

Referee: Wendy THOMS (ENG)   Attendance: 13,524.

Goal: 57' Sandra SMISEK 1-0.

Yellow Card: Anne BUGGE-PAULSEN.

04.07.2001   Donaustadion, Ulm: Denmark – Sweden 0-1 (0-1).

DENMARK: Heidi JOHANSEN, Gitte ANDERSEN, Julie ANDERSSON, Katrine SØNDERGAARD PEDERSEN, Cathrine PAASKE SÖRENSEN (46' Nadia KJAELDGAARD), Christine BONDE, Lene TERP, Christina PETERSEN, Lene JENSEN (46' Lise SØNDERGAARD), Gitte KROGH, Merete PEDERSEN (73' Janne MADSEN). (Coach: Poul HØJMOSE).

SWEDEN: Caroline JÖNSSON, Karolina WESTBERG, Hanna MARKLUND, Sara LARSSON, Malin MOSTRÖM, Tina NORDLUND (78' Victoria SVENSSON), Malin ANDERSSON, Sofia ERIKSSON (46' Kristin BENGTSSON), Linda FAGERSTRÖM, Hanna LJUNGBERG, Therese LUNDIN (63' Therese SJÖGRAN).
(Coach: Marika DOMANSKI-LYFORS).

Referee: Katriina ELOVIRTA (FIN0   Attendance: 6,000.

Goal: 9' Tina NORDLUND 0-1.

Yellow Card: Katrine SØNDERGAARD PEDERSEN.

FINAL

07.07.2001   Donaustadion, Ulm: Germany – Sweden 1-0 (0-0, 0-0).

GERMANY: Silke ROTTENBERG, Kerstin STEGEMANN, Steffi JONES, Doris FITSCHEN, Pia WUNDERLICH, Ariane HINGST, Bettina WIEGMANN, Renate LINGOR, Sandra SMISEK (55' Claudia MÜLLER), Maren MEINERT, Birgit PRINZ.
(Coach: Tina THEUNE).

SWEDEN: Caroline JÖNSSON, Karolina WESTBERG, Hanna MARKLUND, Kristin BENGTSSON, Sara LARSSON, Malin MOSTRÖM, Tina NORDLUND (91' Elin FLYBORG), Malin ANDERSSON, Therese SJÖGRAN (70' Linda FAGERSTRÖM), Hanna LJUNGBERG, Victoria SVENSSON. (Coach: Marika DOMANSKI-LYFORS).

Referee: Nicole PETIGNAT (SUI)   Attendance: 18,000.

Goal: 98' Claudia MÜLLER 1-0.

Yellow Cards: Malin MOSTRÖM, Therese SJÖGRAN.

Germany won following extra time.

Germany were European Champions

UEFA EUROPEAN WOMEN'S CHAMPIONSHIP

EURO 2005

The same format was used like EURO 1997 and 2001. The number 1 and 2 of the group proceed through the semi-finals and the winners through to the final. All matches were played in England.

GROUP A

05.06.2005   Bloomfield Road, Blackpool: Sweden – Denmark 1-1 (1-1).

SWEDEN: Hedvig LINDAHL, Jane TÖRNQVIST, Hanna MARKLUND, Kristin BENGTSSON, Sara LARSSON, Malin MÖSTROM, Frida ÖSTBERG, Caroline SEGER (56' Therese SJÖGRAN), Hanna LJUNGBERG, Victoria SVENSSON, Lotta SCHELIN. (Coach: Marika DOMANSKI-LYFORS).

DENMARK: Tine CEDERKVIST, Bettina FALK, Katrine SØNDERGAARD PEDERSEN (86' Mia BROGAARD), Gitte ANDERSEN, Mariann KNUDSEN, Louise HANSEN, Cathrine PAASKE SÖRENSEN, Anne NIELSEN, Nanna JOHANSEN (86' Lene JENSEN), Merete PEDERSEN, Johanna RASMUSSEN (79' Dorte DALUM). (Coach: Peter BONDE).

Referee: Kari SEITZ (USA)   Attendance: 3,231.

Goals: 20' Hanna LJUNGBERG 1-0, 28' Johanna RASMUSSEN 1-1.

Yellow Cards: Frida ÖSTBERG, Johanna RASMUSSEN.

05.06.2005   City of Manchester Stadium, Manchester: England – Finland 3-2 (2-0).

ENGLAND: Josephine FLETCHER, Alex SCOTT, Rachel UNITT, Faye WHITE (85' Lindsay JOHNSON), Mary PHILLIP, Katie CHAPMAN, Fara WILLIAMS, Kelly SMITH (46' Emily WESTWOOD), Amanda BARR (73' Eniola ALUKO), Rachel YANKEY, Karen CARNEY. (Coach: Hope POWELL).

FINLAND: Satu KUNNAS, Petra VAELMA, Sanna VALKONEN, Tiina SALMÉN, Eveliina SARAPÄÄ, Jessica JULIN, Anna MÄKINEN, Anna-Kaisa RANTANEN, Laura KALMARI, Heidi KACKUR (81' Sanna TALONEN), Jessica THORN (74' Minna MUSTONEN). (Coach: Not known).

Referee: Gyöngyi GAÁL (HUN)   Attendance: 29,092.

Goals: 18' Sanna VALKONEN 1-0 (og), 40' Amanda BARR 2-0,
56' Anna-Kaisa RANTANEN 2-1, 89' Laura KALMARI 2-2, 90' Karen CARNEY 3-2.

Yellow Card: Heidi KACKUR.

08.06.2005   Ewood Park, Blackburn: Denmark – England 2-1 (0-0).

DENMARK: Tine CEDERKVIST, Bettina FALK, Katrine SØNDERGAARD PEDERSEN, Gitte ANDERSEN, Mariann KNUDSEN, Louise HANSEN, Cathrine PAASKE SÖRENSEN, Anne NIELSEN (71' Tanja CHRISTENSEN), Nanna JOHANSEN (57' Lene JENSEN), Merete PEDERSEN, Johanna RASMUSSEN. (Coach: Peter BONDE).

ENGLAND: Josephine FLETCHER, Alex SCOTT, Rachel UNITT, Faye WHITE, Mary PHILLIP, Katie CHAPMAN, Fara WILLIAMS, Kelly SMITH (46' Vicky EXLEY), Amanda BARR (64' Eniola ALUKO), Rachel YANKEY, Karen CARNEY. (Coach: Hope POWELL).

Referee: Alexandra IHRINGOVÁ (ENG)   Attendance: 14,695.

Goals: 52' Fara WILLIAMS 0-1 (p), 80' Merete PEDERSEN 1-1, 88' Cathrine PAASKE SÖRENSEN 2-1.

Yellow Cards: Katie CHAMPMAN, Fara WILLIAMS, Kelly SMITH.

08.06.2005   Bloomfield Road, Blackpool: Sweden – Finland 0-0.

SWEDEN: Hedvig LINDAHL, Jane TÖRNQVIST, Hanna MARKLUND, Kristin BENGTSSON, Sara LARSSON, Malin MÖSTROM, Malin ANDERSSON, Therese SJÖGRAN (71' Anna SJÖSTRÖM), Hanna LJUNGBERG, Victoria SVENSSON, Lotta SCHELIN (56' Josefine ÖQVIST). (Coach: Marika DOMANSKI-LYFORS).

FINLAND: Satu KUNNAS, Petra VAELMA, Sanna VALKONEN, Tiina SALMÉN, Eveliina SARAPÄÄ, Jessica JULIN, Anna MÄKINEN, Ninna MUSTONEN (71' Sanna TALONEN), Anna-Kaisa RANTANEN (90' Sanna MALASKA), Laura KALMARI, Heidi KACKUR (46' Jessica THORN). (Coach: Not known).

Referee: Dagmar DAMKOVÁ (CZE)   Attendance: 1,491.

Yellow Card: Jessica JULIN.

11.06.2005   Ewood Park, Blackburn: England – Sweden 0-1 (0-1).

ENGLAND: Rachel BROWN-FINNIS, Alex SCOTT, Rachel UNITT, Faye WHITE, Mary PHILLIP, Katie CHAPMAN, Fara WILLIAMS, Kelly SMITH, Rachel YANKEY, Karen CARNEY (69' Amanda BARR), Eniola ALUKO. (Coach: Hope POWELL).

SWEDEN: Hedvig LINDAHL, Jane TÖRNQVIST, Hanna MARKLUND, Kristin BENGTSSON, Sara LARSSON, Malin MÖSTROM, Therese SJÖGRAN, Caroline SEGER (54' Frida ÖSTBERG), Anna SJÖSTRÖM, Hanna LJUNGBERG, Victoria SVENSSON (90' Josefine ÖQVIST). (Coach: Marika DOMANSKI-LYFORS).

Referee: Nicole PETIGNAT (SUI)   Attendance: 25,694.

Goal: 3' Anna SJÖSTRÖM 0-1.

Yellow Cards: Kelly SMITH, Rachel YANKEY, Jane TÖRNQVIST, Malin MÖSTROM, Caroline SEGER.

11.06.2005   Bloomfield Road, Blackpool: Finland – Denmark 2-1 (2-1).

FINLAND: Satu KUNNAS, Petra VAELMA, Sanna VALKONEN, Tiina SALMÉN, Eveliina SARAPÄÄ, Jessica JULIN, Anna MÄKINEN, Anna-Kaisa RANTANEN, Laura KALMARI (89' Minna MUSTONEN), Heidi KACKUR (74' Heidi LINDSTRÖM), Jessica THORN (59' Sanna MALASKA). (Coach: Not known).

DENMARK: Tine CEDERKVIST, Katrine SØNDERGAARD PEDERSEN, Gitte ANDERSEN, Dorte DALUM, Mia BROGAARD (70' Helle NIELSEN), Louise HANSEN (70' Tanja CHRISTENSEN), Cathrine PAASKE SØRENSEN, Anne NIELSEN, Nanna JOHANSEN (63' Stine JENSEN), Merete PEDERSEN, Johanna RASMUSSEN. (Coach: Peter BONDE).

Referee: Alexandra IHRINGOVÁ (ENG)   Attendance: 1,481.

Goals: 6' Laura KALMARI 1-0, 16' Heidi KACKUR 2-0, 45' Cathrine PAASKE SØRENSEN 2-1.

Yellow Card: Cathrine PAASKE SØRENSEN.

FINAL STANDINGS

1.	SWEDEN	3	1	2	0	2	-	1	5
2.	DENMARK	3	1	1	1	4	-	4	4
3.	FINLAND	3	1	1	1	4	-	4	4
4.	ENGLAND	3	1	0	2	4	-	5	3

GROUP B

06.06.2005   Halliwell Jones Stadium, Warrington: Germany – Norway 1-0 (0-0).

GERMANY: Silke ROTTENBERG, Kerstin STEGEMANN, Steffi JONES, Sandra MINNERT, Ariane HINGST, Renate LINGOR, Kerstin GAREFREKES, Navina OMILADE-KELLER (62' Britta CARLSON), Inka GRINGS (71' Sandra SMISEK), Anja MITTAG, Conny POHLERS (80' Petra WIMBERSKY).   (Coach: Tina THEUNE).

NORWAY: Bente NORDBY, Ane HORPESTAD, Gunhild FØLSTAD, Marit CHRISTENSEN, Marianne PAULSEN, Ingvild STENSLAND, Solveig GULBRANDSEN, Unni LEHN (66' Lise KLAVENESS), Trine BJERKE RØNNING, Dagny MELLGREN, Stine FRANTZEN (83' Isabell HERLOVSEN).   (Coach: Bjarne BERNTSEN).

Referee: Nicole PETIGNAT (SUI)   Attendance: 1,600.

Goal: 61' Conny POHLERS 1-0.

Yellow Cards: Renate LINGOR, Unni LEHN, Stine FRANTZEN, Lise KLAVENESS.

06.06.2005   Deepdale, Preston: France – Italy 3-1 (3-0).

FRANCE: Sarah BOUHADDI, Corinne DIACRE, Laura GEORGES, Sandrine DUSANG (90' Peggy PROVOST), Anne-Laure CASSELEUX, Sandrine SOUBEYRAND, Sonia BOMPASTOR, Élise BUSSAGLIA, Stephanie MUGNERET-BEGHE, Marinette PICHON (85' Camille ABILY), Hoda LATTAF (72' ÉLODIE THOMIS).   (Coach: Elisabeth LOISEL).

ITALY: Carla BRUNOZZI, Elisabette TONA, Gioia MASIA (39' Elena FICARELLI), Viviana SCHIAVI, Tatiana ZORRI, Sara DI FILIPPO, Chiara GAZZOLI (46' Melania GABBIADINI), Elisa CAMPORESE, Pamela CONTI (69' Giulia DOMENICHETTI), Patrizia PANICO, Ilaria PASQUI.   (Coach: Not known).

Referee: Wendy THOMS (ENG)   Attendance: 957.

Goals: 16' Hoda LATTAF 1-0, 20', 30' Marinette PICHON 2-0, 3-0,
83' Sara DI FILIPPO 3-1.

Yellow Cards: Sandrine SOUBEYRAND, Gioia MASIA, Pamela CONTI, Patrizia PANICO.

09.06.2005   Deepdale, Preston: Italy – Germany 0-4 (0-2).

ITALY: Carla BRUNOZZI, Elisabette TONA, Gioia MASIA, Viviana SCHIAVI (46' Damiana DE LANA), Elena FICARELLI, Tatiana ZORRI (75' Valentina BONI), Sara DI FILIPPO, Elisa CAMPORESE, Pamela CONTI (51' Giulia DOMENICHETTI), Patrizia PANICO, Ilaria PASQUI. (Coach: Not known).

GERMANY: Silke ROTTENBERG, Kerstin STEGEMANN (19' Inka GRINGS), Steffi JONES, Sandra MINNERT, Ariane HINGST, Renate LINGOR, Britta CARLSON, Kerstin GAREFREKES, Birgit PRINZ, Anja MITTAG (77' Sandra SMISEK), Conny POHLERS. (Coach: Tina THEUNE).

Referee: Kari SEITZ (USA)   Attendance: 1,497.

Goals: 11' Birgit PRINZ 0-1, 18' Conny POHLERS 0-2, 55' Steffi JONES 0-3, 74' Anja MITTAG 0-4.

Yellow Cards: Gioia MASIA, Sara DI FILIPPO, Elisa CAMPORESE, Conny POHLERS.

Anja Mittag missed a penalty in the 74th minute.

09.06.2005   Halliwell Jones Stadium, Warrington: France – Norway 1-1 (1-0).

FRANCE: Sarah BOUHADDI, Corinne DIACRE, Laura GEORGES, Sandrine DUSANG, Peggy PROVOST, Sandrine SOUBEYRAND, Sonia BOMPASTOR, Élise BUSSAGLIA, Stephanie MUGNERET-BEGHE (54' Marie-Ange KRAMO), Marinette PICHON, Hoda LATTAF. (Coach: Elisabeth LOISEL).

NORWAY: Bente NORDBY, Ane HORPESTAD, Gunhild FØLSTAD, Siri NORDBY, Marit CHRISTENSEN, Ingvild STENSLAND, Solveig GULBRANDSEN, Unni LEHN (46' Isabell HERLOVSEN), Trine BJERKE RØNNING, Dagny MELLGREN, Stine FRANTZEN (64' Lise KLAVENESS).   (Coach: Bjarne BERNTSEN).

Referee: Gyöngyi GAÁL (HUN)   Attendance: 3,263.

Goals: 20' Stephanie MUGNERET-BEGHE 1-0, 66' Isabell HERLOVSEN 1-1.

12.06.2005   Halliwell Jones Stadium, Warrington: Germany – France 3-0 (0-0).

GERMANY: Silke ROTTENBERG, Steffi JONES, Sandra MINNERT, Ariane HINGST, Renate LINGOR (80' Britta CARLSON), Kerstin GAREFREKES, Navina OMILADE-KELLER, Inka GRINGS, Birgit PRINZ, Anja MITTAG (46' Sonja FUSS), Conny POHLERS (46' Pia WUNDERLICH). (Coach: Tina THEUNE).

FRANCE: Sarah BOUHADDI, Corinne DIACRE, Laura GEORGES, Sandrine DUSANG, Peggy PROVOST, Sandrine SOUBEYRAND, Sonia BOMPASTOR, Camille ABILY, Louisa CADAMURO, Stephanie MUGNERET-BEGHE (32' Marie-Ange KRAMO), Marinette PICHON (80' Candie HERBERT).   (Coach: Elisabeth LOISEL).

Referee: Floarea BABADAC (ROM)   Attendance: 3,835.

Goals: 72' Inka GRINGS 1-0, 77' Renate LINGOR 2-0, 83' Sandra MINNERT 3-0.

Yellow Cards: Navina OMILADE-KELLER, Sarah BOUHADDI, Marie-Ange KRAMO.

12.06.2005   Deepdale, Preston: Norway – Italy 5-3 (4-1).

NORWAY: Bente NORDBY, Ane HORPESTAD, Gunhild FØLSTAD, Marit CHRISTENSEN, Marianne PAULSEN, Ingvild STENSLAND, Solveig GULBRANDSEN (69' Marie KNUTSEN), Lise KLAVENESS, Trine BJERKE RØNNING (46' Unni LEHN), Isabell HERLOVSEN (83' Stine FRANTZEN), Dagny MELLGREN.
(Coach: Bjarne BERNTSEN).

ITALY: Carla BRUNOZZI, Elisabette TONA, Valentina LANZIERI (63' Damiana DE LANA), Elena FICARELLI, Tatiana ZORRI, Elisa CAMPORESE, Pamela CONTI, Giulia DOMENICHETTI (554' Valentina BONI), Patrizia PANICO, Ilaria PASQUI (90' Viviana SCHIAVI), Melania GABBIADINI.   (Coach: Not known).

Referee: Dagmar DAMKOVÁ (CZE)   Attendance: 1,154.

Goals: 7' Lise KLAVENESS 1-0, 8' Melania GABBIADINI 1-1, 29' Marit CHRISTENSEN 2-1, 35' Solveig GULBRANDSEN 3-1, 44' Dagny MELLGREN 4-1, 53' Melania GABBIADINI 4-2, 57' Lise KLAVENESS 5-2, 69' Elisa CAMPORESE 5-3.

Yellow Cards: Elisa CAMPORESE, Pamela CONTI.

FINAL STANDINGS

1.	GERMANY	3	3	0	0	8	-	0	9
2.	NORWAY	3	1	1	1	6	-	5	4
3.	FRANCE	3	1	1	1	4	-	5	4
4.	ITALY	3	0	0	3	4	-	12	0

SEMI-FINALS

15.06.2005   Deepdale, Preston: Germany – Finland 4-1 (3-1).

GERMANY: Silke ROTTENBERG, Steffi JONES, Sandra MINNERT, Ariane HINGST, Renate LINGOR (75' Sarah GÜNTHER-WERLEIN), Britta CARLSON, Kerstin GAREFREKES (62' Petra WIMBERSKY), Inka GRINGS, Birgit PRINZ, Anja MITTAG (46' Sonja FUSS), Conny POHLERS. (Coach: Tina THEUNE).

FINLAND: Satu KUNNAS, Petra VAELMA, Sanna VALKONEN, Tiina SALMÉN, Eveliina SARAPÄÄ (69' Jessica THORN), Jessica JULIN (81' Sanna MALASKA), Anna MÄKINEN, Anna-Kaisa RANTANEN, Laura KALMARI, Minna MUSTONEN (46' Terhi UUSI-LUOMALAHTI), Heidi KACKUR. (Coach: Not known).

Referee: Dagmar DAMKOVÁ (CZE)   Attendance: 2,785.

Goals: 3' Inka GRINGS 1-0, 8' Conny POHLERS 2-0, 12' Inka GRINGS 3-0, 15' Minna MUSTONEN 3-1, 62' Birgir PRINZ 4-1.

Yellow Card: Tiina SALMÉN

16.06.2005   Halliwell Jones Stadium, Warrington: Sweden – Norway 2-3 (1-1, 2-2).

SWEDEN: Hedvig LINDAHL, Jane TÖRNQVIST, Hanna MARKLUND, Kristin BENGTSSON, Sara LARSSON, Malin MÖSTROM, Therese SJÖGRAN (71' Josefine ÖQVIST), Caroline SEGER (46' Frida ÖSTBERG), Anna SJÖSTRÖM, Hanna LJUNGBERG, Victoria SVENSSON (49' Lotta SCHELIN). (Coach: Marika DOMANSKI-LYFORS).

NORWAY: Bente NORDBY, Ane HORPESTAD, Gunhild FØLSTAD, Marit CHRISTENSEN (83' Maritha KAUFMANN), Marianne PAULSEN, Ingvild STENSLAND, Solveig GULBRANDSEN, Unni LEHN (60' Trine BJERKE RØNNING), Lise KLAVENESS, Isabell HERLOVSEN (65' Stine FRANTZEN), Dagny MELLGREN.
(Coach: Bjarne BERNTSEN).

Referee: Kari SEITZ (USA)   Attendance: 5,722.

Goals: 41' Solveig GULBRANDSEN 0-1, 43' Hanna LJUNGBERG 1-1, 65' Isabell HERLOVSEN 1-2, 89' Hanna LJUNGBERG 2-2, 109' Solveig GULBRANDSEN 2-3.

Yellow Card: Solveig GULBRANDSEN.

Norway won following extra-time.

FINAL

19.06.2005 Ewood Park, Blackburn: Germany – Norway 3-1 (2-1).

GERMANY: Silke ROTTENBERG, Steffi JONES, Sandra MINNERT, Ariane HINGST, Renate LINGOR, Britta CARLSON (81' Sarah GÜNTHER-WERLEIN), Kerstin GAREFREKES, Inka GRINGS (68' Sandra SMISEK), Birgit PRINZ, Anja MITTAG (59' Petra WIMBERSKY), Conny POHLERS. (Coach: Tina THEUNE).

NORWAY: Bente NORDBY, Ane HORPESTAD, Gunhild FØLSTAD, Marit CHRISTENSEN, Marianne PAULSEN, Ingvild STENSLAND, Solveig GULBRANDSEN, Lise KLAVENESS (87' Kristin BLYSTAD BJERKE), Trine BJERKE RØNNING (83' Marie KNUTSEN), Dagny MELLGREN, Stine FRANTZEN (59' Isabell HERLOVSEN). (Coach: Bjarne BERNTSEN).

Referee: Alexandra IHRINGOVÁ (ENG)   Attendance: 21,105.

Goals: 21' Inka GRINGS 1-0, 24' Renate LINGOR 2-0, 41' Dagny MELLGREN 2-1, 63' Birgit PRINZ 3-1.

Germany were European Champions

UEFA EUROPEAN WOMEN'S CHAMPIONSHIP
EURO 2009

The fomat was different from the previous tournaments.
The number 1 and 2 of each group, together with the 2 best number 3 countries proceed to the quarter-finals. All matches were played in Finland.

GROUP A

23.08.2009   Veritas, Turku: Ukraine – Netherlands 0-2 (0-2).

UKRAINE: Nadiya BARANOVA, Olena MAZURENKO, Olena KHODYRYEVA, Alla LYSHAFAY, Tetyana CHORNA, Lyudmyla PEKUR, Vera DJATEL (83' Iryna VASYLYUK), Nataliya ZINCHENKO, Natalya SUKHORUKOVA (46' Oksana YAKOVISHYN), Olga BOYCHENKO, Daryna APANASCHENKO.   (Coach: Not known).

NETHERLANDS: Loes GEURTS, Dyanne BITO, Daphne KOSTER, Manoe MEULEN, Petra HOGEWONING, Anouk HOOGENDIJK, Annemieke KIESEL, Kirsten VAN DE VEN (79' Marlous PIEËTE), Manon MELIS, Karin STEVENS (86' Chantal DE RIDDER), Sylvia SMIT.   (Coach: Vera PAUW).

Referee: Cristina DORCIOMAN (ROM)   Attendance: 2,671.

Goals: 4' Kirsten VAN DE VEN 0-1, 9' Karin STEVENS 0-2.

Yellow Cards: Lyudmila PEKUR, Vera DJATEL, Olgs BOYCHENKO, Petra HOGEWONING.

23.08.2009   Olympiastadion, Helsinki: Finland – Denmark 1-0 (0-0).

FINLAND: Tinja-Riikka KORPELA, Petra VAELMA, Sanna VALKONEN, Tiina SALMÉN, Maija SAARI, Jessica JULIN (84' Annica SJÖLUND), Anne MÄKINEN, Anna WESTERLUND, Essi SAINIO (60' Sanna TALONEN), Laura KALMARI, Linda SÄLLSTROM (73' Susanna LEHTINEN). (Coach: Michael KÄLD).

DENMARK: Heidi JOHANSEN, Katrine SØNDERGAARD PEDERSEN, Line RØDDIK, Camilla SAND, Mia BROGAARD, Mette JENSEN (72' Nadia NADIM), Cathrine PAASKE SØRENSEN, Julie RYDAHL (89' Marianne LØTH), Tina KAERGAARD (46' Katrine VEJE), Maikne PAPE, Johanna RASMUSSEN.   (Coach: Kenneth HEINER-MØLLER).

Referee: Dagmar DAMKOVÁ (CZE)   Attendance: 16,324.

Goal: 49' Maija SAARI 1-0.

Yellow Card: Anna WESTERLUND.

26.08.2009   Finnair Stadium, Helsinki: Ukraine – Denmark 1-2 (0-0).

UKRAINE: Nadiya BARANOVA, Olena MAZURENKO, Olena KHODYRYEVA, Inesa TITOVA, Alla LYSHAFAY, Tetyana CHORNA, Lyudmyla PEKUR, Vera DJATEL, Nataliya ZINCHENKO, Oksana YAKOVISHYN, Daryna APANASCHENKO (64' Olga BOYCHENKO). (Coach: Not known).

DENMARK: Heidi JOHANSEN, Katrine SØNDERGAARD PEDERSEN, Line RØDDIK, Camilla SAND, Mia BROGAARD, Mette JENSEN, Cathrine PAASKE SØRENSEN, Julie RYDAHL, Maiken PAPE, Nadia NADIM (56' Katrine VEJE), Johanna RASMUSSEN (90' Lene JENSEN). (Coach: Kenneth HEINER-MØLLER).

Referee: Gyöngyi GAÁL (HUN)   Attendance: 1,372.

Goals: 49' Camilla SAND 0-1, 63' Daryna APANASCHENKO 1-1, 87' Maiken PAPE 1-2.

Yellow Cards: Olena KHODYRYEVA, Tetyana CHORNA.

26.08.2009   Olympiastadion, Helsinki: Finland – Netherlands 2-1 (1-1).

FINLAND: Tinja-Riikka KORPELA, Petra VAELMA, Sanna VALKONEN, Tiina SALMÉN, Maija SAARI, Jessica JULIN (78' Anna-Kaisa RANTANEN), Anne MÄKINEN, Anna WESTERLUND (46' Annica SJÖLUND), Essi SAINIO, Laura KALMARI, Linda SÄLLSTROM. (Coach: Michael KÄLD).

NETHERLANDS: Loes GEURTS, Dyanne BITO, Daphne KOSTER, Manoe MEULEN, Petra HOGEWONING, Anouk HOOGENDIJK, Annemieke KIESEL, Kirsten VAN DE VEN, Manon MELIS, Karin STEVENS (68' Chantal DE RIDDER), Sylvia SMIT. (Coach: Vera PAUW).

Referee: Jenny PALMQVIST (SWE)   Attendance: 16,148.

Goals: 7' Laura KALMARI 1-0, 25' Kirsten VAN DE VEN 1-1, 69' Laura KALMARI 2-1.

29.08.2009   Lahden, Lahti: Denmark – Netherlands 1-2 (0-0).

DENMARK: Heidi JOHANSEN, Katrine SØNDERGAARD PEDERSEN, Line RØDDIK, Camilla SAND, Mia BROGAARD, Cathrine PAASKE SØRENSEN, Julie RYDAHL, Maiken PAPE, Nadia NADIM (46' Katrine VEJE), Johanna RASMUSSEN, Sanne TROELSGAARD-NIELSEN (72' Marianne LØTH). (Coach: Kenneth HEINER-MØLLER).

NETHERLANDS: Loes GEURTS, Dyanne BITO, Daphne KOSTER, Manoe MEULEN, Petra HOGEWONING, Anouk HOOGENDIJK, Annemieke KIESEL, Kirsten VAN DE VEN (75' Claudia VAN DEN HEILIGENBERG), Chantal DE RIDDER (46' Kaarin STEVENS), Manon MELIS, Sylvia SMIT (90' Marlous PIEËTE). (Coach: Vera PAUW).

Referee: Jenny PALMQVIST (SWE)   Attendance: 1,712.

Goals: 58' Sylvia SMIT 0-1, 66' Manon MELIS 0-2, 71' Johanna RASMUSSEN 1-2.

Yellow Cards: Julie RYDAHL, Karin STEVENS.

29.08.2009   Olympiastadion, Helsinki: Finland – Ukraine 0-1 (0-0).

FINLAND: Minna MERILUOTO, Petra VAELMA, Tiina SALMÉN (58' Miia NIEMI), Tuija HYYRYNEN, Maija SAARI, Jessica JULIN, Anne MÄKINEN (46' Linda SÄLLSTROM), Katri NOKSO-KOIVISTO (54' Sanna TALONEN), Anna-Kaisa RANTANEN, Laura KALMARI, Annica SJÖLUND. (Coach: Michael KÄLD).

UKRAINE: Iryna ZVARYCH (39' Nadiya BARANOVA), Olena MAZURENKO, Olena KHODYRYEVA, Yuliya VASHCHENKO (85' Iryna VASYLYUK), Alla LYSHAFAY, Tetyana CHORNA, Lyudmyla PEKUR, Vera DJATEL, Nataliya ZINCHENKO, Oksana YAKOVISHYN (77' Olga BOYCHENKO), Daryna APANASCHENKO. (Coach: Not known).

Referee: Natalia AVDONCHENKO (RUS)   Attendance: 15,138.

Goal: Lyudmyla PEKUR 0-1.

Yellow Card: Petra VAELMA.

FINAL STANDINGS

1.	NETHERLANDS	3	2	0	1	5 - 3	6
2.	FINLAND	3	2	0	1	3 - 2	6
3.	DENMARK	3	1	0	2	3 - 4	3
4.	UKRAINE	3	1	0	2	2 - 4	3

GROUP B

24.08.2009   Ratina, Tampere: Germany – Norway 4-0 (1-0).

GERMANY: Nadine ANGERER, Babett PETER, Annike KRAHN, Ariane HINGST, Bianca SCHMIDT, Melanie BEHRINGER (86' Anja MTTAG), Linda BRESONIK, Kim KULIG-SOYAH, Kerstin GAREFREKES (65' Célia ŠAŠIĆ), Inka GRINGS (65' Fatmire ALUSHI), Birgit PRINZ.   (Coach: Silvia NEID).

NORWAY: Ingrid HJELMSETH, Toril AKERHAUGEN, Camilla HUSE, Maren MJELDE, Ingvidl STENSLAND, Solveig GULBRANDSEN, Lene STORLØKKEN (80' Anneli GISKE), Trine BJERKE RØNNING, Isabell HERLOVSEN, Melissa WIIK (72' Cecilie PEDERSEN), Elise THORSNES (58' Leni KAURIN).   (Coach: Bjarne BERNTSEN).

Referee: Alexandra IHRINGOVÁ (ENG)   Attendance: 6,552.

Goals: 33' Linda BRESONIK 1-0 (p), 89' Fatmire ALUSHI 2-0, 90' Anja MITTAG 3-0, 90' Fatmire ALUSHI 4-0.

Yellow Cards: Linda BRESONIK, Kim KULIG-SOYAH, Maren MJELDE.

24.08.2009   Ratina, Tampere: Iceland – France 1-3 (1-1).

ICELAND: Þóra HELGADÓTTIR, Gudrún GUNNARSDÓTTIR, Ólina VIDARSDÓTTIR, Katrin JÓNSDÓTTIR, Erna SIGURDARDÓTTIR, Edda GARDARSDÓTTIR, Hólmfridur MAGNÚSDÓTTIR (89' Fanndis FRIDRIKSDÓTTIR), Dóra Maria LÁRUSDÓTTIR, Sara Björk GUNNARSDÓTTIR (76' Erla ARNARDÓTTIR), Katrin OMARSDÓTTIR (71' Rakel HÖNNUDÓTTIR), Margrét Lára VIDARSDÓTTIR.   (Coach: Sigurdur EYJÓLFSSON).

FRANCE: Sarah BOUHADDI, Ophélie MEILLEROUX, Laura GEORGES, Sandrine SOUBEYRAND, Corine PETIT (37' Sabrina VIGUIER), Sonia BOMPASTOR, Camille ABILY, Louisa CADAMURO, Élise BUSSAGLIA, Candie HERBERT (40' Sandrine BRÉTIGNY), Élodie THOMIS (86' Eugénie LE SOMMER).   (Coach: Bruno BINI).

Referee: Natalia AVDONCHENKO (RUS)   Attendance: 1,460.

Goals: 6' Hólmfridur MAGNÚSDÓTTIR 1-0, 18' Camille ABILY 1-1 (p), 53' Sonia BOMPASTOR 1-2 (p), 67' Louisa CADAMURO 1-3.

Yellow Cards: Ólina VIDARSDÓTTIR, Élodie THOMIS

Margrét Lára Vidarsdóttir missed a penalty in the 77th minute.

27.08.2009   Ratina, Tampere: France – Germany 1-5 (0-3).

FRANCE: Sarah BOUHADDI, Ophélie MEILLEROUX, Laura GEORGES, Sabrina VIGUIER (69' Laure LEPAILLEUR), Sandrine SOUBEYRAND, Sonia BOMPASTOR, Camille ABILY, Louisa CADAMURO (68' Eugénie LE SOMMER), Élise BUSSAGLIA (79' Sandrine BRÉTIGNY), Gaëtane THINEY, Élodie THOMIS. (Coach: Bruno BINI).

GERMANY: Nadine ANGERER, Babett PETER, Annike KRAHN, Ariane HINGST, Bianca SCHMIDT, Melanie BEHRINGER (46' Simone LAUDEHR), Linda BRESONIK, Kim KULIG-SOYAH (66' Sasia BARTUSIAK), Kerstin GAREFREKES, Inka GRINGS (77' Célia ŠAŠIĆ), Birgit PRINZ. (Coach: Silvia NEID).

Referee: Kateryna MONZUL (UKR)   Attendance: 3,331.

Goals: 9' Inka GRINGS 0-1, 17' Annika KRAHN 0-2, 45' Melanie BEHRINGER 0-3, 47' Linda BRESONIK 0-4 (p), 51' Gaëtane THINEY 1-4, 90' Simone LAUDEHR 1-5.

Yellow Cards: Sonia BOMPASTOR, Saskia BARTUSIAK.

27.08.2009   Lahden, Lahti: Iceland – Norway 0-1 (0-1).

ICELAND: Þóra HELGADÓTTIR, Gudrún GUNNARSDÓTTIR, Ólina VIDARSDÓTTIR, Katrin JÓNSDÓTTIR, Erna SIGURDARDÓTTIR (82' Rakel HÖNNUDÓTTIR), Edda GARDARSDÓTTIR, Hólmfridur MAGNÚSDÓTTIR, Dóra STEFÁNSDÓTTIR (60' Rakel LOGADÓTTIR), Dóra Maria LÁRUSDÓTTIR, Sara Björk GUNNARSDÓTTIR, Margrét Lára VIDARSDÓTTIR. (Coach: Sigurdur EYJÓLFSSON).

NORWAY: Ingrid HJELMSETH, Toril AKERHAUGEN, Camilla HUSE, Maren MJELDE, Ingvidl STENSLAND, Anneli GISKE, Solveig GULBRANDSEN, Lene STORLØKKEN, Trine BJERKE RØNNING, Isabell HERLOVSEN (86' Ingvild ISAKSEN), Cecilie PEDERSEN (90' Kristin LIE). (Coach: Bjarne BERNTSEN).

Referee: Cristina DORCIOMAN (ROM)   Attendance: 1,399.

Goal: 45' Cecilie PEDERSEN 0-1.

Yellow Card: Trine BJERKE RØNNING.

30.08.2009   Ratina, Tampere: Germany – Iceland 1-0 (0-0).

GERMANY: Nadine ANGERER, Saskia BARTUSIAK, Babett PETER, Annike KRAHN, Sonja FUSS (46' Kerstin STEGEMANN), Ariane HINGST, Simone LAUDEHR, Fatmire ALUSHI, Birgit PRINZ (46' Inka GRINGS / 59' Célia ŠAŠIĆ), Anja MITTAG, Martina MÜLLER. (Coach: Silvia NEID).

ICELAND: Gudbjörg GUNNARSDÓTTIR, Gudrún GUNNARSDÓTTIR, Ólina VIDARSDÓTTIR, Katrin JÓNSDÓTTIR, Sif ATLADÓTTIR, Edda GARDARSDÓTTIR, Hólmfridur MAGNÚSDÓTTIR (71' Rakel HÖNNUDÓTTIR), Dóra Maria LÁRUSDÓTTIR (71' Erla ARNARDÓTTIR), Sara Björk GUNNARSDÓTTIR, Katrin OMARSDÓTTIR (87' Fanndis FRIDRIKSDÓTTIR), Margrét Lára VIDARSDÓTTIR.
(Coach: Sigurdur EYJÓLFSSON).

Referee: Kirsi HEIKKINEN (FIN)   Attendance: 3,101.

Goal: 50' Inka GRINGS 1-0.

Yellow Card: Sif ATLADÓTTIR.

30.08.2009   Olympiastadion, Helsinki: Norway – France 1-1 (1-1).

NORWAY: Ingrid HJELMSETH, Toril AKERHAUGEN, Camilla HUSE, Maren MJELDE, Ingvidl STENSLAND, Anneli GISKE, Solveig GULBRANDSEN, Lene STORLØKKEN, Trine BJERKE RØNNING, Isabell HERLOVSEN (89' Melissa WIIK), Cecilie PEDERSEN (46' Leni KAURIN). (Coach: Bjarne BERNTSEN).

FRANCE: Sarah BOUHADDI, Ophélie MEILLEROUX, Laura GEORGES, Delphine BLANC, Sandrine SOUBEYRAND, Sonia BOMPASTOR, Camille ABILY, Louisa CADAMURO, Élise BUSSAGLIA, Gaëtane THINEY (83' Eugénie LE SOMMER), Élodie THOMIS. (Coach: Bruno BINI).

Referee: Alexandra IHRINGOVÁ (ENG)   Attendance: 1,537.

Goals: 4' Lene STORLØKKEN 1-0, 16' Camille ABILY 1-1.

FINAL STANDINGS

1.	GERMANY	3	3	0	0	10	-	1	9
2.	FRANCE	3	1	1	1	5	-	7	4
3.	NORWAY	3	1	1	1	2	-	5	4
4.	ICELAND	3	0	0	3	1	-	5	0

GROUP C

25.08.2009   Lahden, Lahti: England – Italy 1-2 (1-0).

ENGLAND: Rachel BROWN-FINNIS, Alex SCOTT, Casey STONEY, Faye WHITE, Fara WILLIAMS, Anita ASANTE (73' Rachel UNITT), Katie CHAPMAN, Jill SCOTT, Karen CARNEY, Eniola ALUKO (46' Kelly SMITH), Sue SMITH (85' Lianne SANDERSON). (Coach: Hope POWELL).

ITALY: Anna PICARELLI, Sara GAMA, Roberta D'ADDA, Elisabetta TONA, Viviana SCHIAVI, Alessia TUTTINO, Tatiana ZORRI, Carolina PINI (77' Alia GUAGNI), Giulia DOMENICHETTI (53' Alice PARSI), Melania GABBIADINI (90' Raffaela MANIERI), Patrizia PANICO. (Coach: Pietro GHEDIN).

Referee: Bibiana STEINHAUS (GER)   Attendance: 2,950.

Goals: 38' Fara WILLIAMS 1-0 (p), 56' Patrizia PANICO 1-1, 81' Alessia TUTTINO 1-2.

Yellow Cards: Fara WILLIAMS, Roberta D'ADDA.

Red card: 28' Casey STONEY.

25.08.2009   Veritas, Turku: Sweden – Russia 3-0 (2-0).

SWEDEN: Hedvig LINDAHL, Charlotte ROHLIN, Anna PAULSON, Sara THUNEBRO, Sara LARSSON, Caroline SEGER, Kosovare ASLLANI (76' Lina NILSSON), Therese SJÖGRAN, Lisa DAHLKVIST (69' Linnea LILJEGÄRD), Lotta SCHELIN, Victoria SVENSSON (87' Nilla FISCHER).   (Coach: Thomas DENNERBY).

RUSSIA: Elena KOCHNEVA, Oksana SHMACHKOVA, Olga PORYADINA, Natalia PERTSEVA, Ksenia TSYBUTOVICH, Tatiana SKOTNIKOVA (87' Nadezhda KHARCHENKO), Valentina SAVCHENKOVA, Elena FOMINA, Elena MOROZOVA, Olesya KUROCHKINA (46' Elena DANILOVA), Olga PETROVA (62' Elena TEREKHOVA).   (Coach: Igor SHALIMOV).

Referee: Kirsi HEIKKINEN (FIN)   Attendance: 4,697.

Goals: 5' Charlotte ROHLIN 1-0, 15' Victoria SVENSSON 2-0, 82' Caroline SEGER 3-0.

28.08.2009   Veritas, Turku: Italy – Sweden 0-2 (0-2).

ITALY: Anna PICARELLI, Sara GAMA, Roberta D'ADDA, Elisabetta TONA, Viviana SCHIAVI, Alessia TUTTINO, Tatiana ZORRI (75' Alice PARISI), Carolina PINI, Giulia DOMENICHETTI, Melania GABBIADINI (69' Silvia FUSELLI), Patrizia PANICO. (Coach: Pietro GHEDIN).

SWEDEN: Hedvig LINDAHL, Charlotte ROHLIN, Stina SEGERSTRÖM, Anna PAULSON, Sara THUNEBRO, Caroline SEGER, Kosovare ASLLANI (79' Linnea LILJEGÄRD), Therese SJÖGRAN (89' Louise SCHILLGARD), Lisa DAHLKVIST (66' Nilla FISCHER), Lotta SCHELIN, Victoria SVENSSON. (Coach: Thomas DENNERBY).

Referee: Bibiana STEINHAUS (GER)   Attendance: 5,947.

Goals: 9' Lotta SCHELIN 0-1, 19' Kosovare ASLLANI 0-2.

Yellow Card: Nilla FISCHER.

28.08.2009   Finnair Stadium, Helsinki: England – Russia 3-2 (3-2).

ENGLAND: Rachel BROWN-FINNIS, Alex SCOTT, Lindsay JOHNSON, Faye WHITE, Rachel UNITT, Fara WILLIAMS, Katie CHAPMAN, Kelly SMITH, Karen CARNEY, Eniola ALUKO, Sue SMITH (66' Jess CLARKE). (Coach: Hope POWELL).

RUSSIA: Elena KOCHNEVA, Oksana SHMACHKOVA, Olga PORYADINA (90' Nadezhda MYSKIV), Natalia PERTSEVA, Ksenia TSYBUTOVICH, Tatiana SKOTNIKOVA, Valentina SAVCHENKOVA, Elena FOMINA (76' Natalia BARBASHINA), Elena MOROZOVA, Olesya KUROCHKINA, Elena DANILOVA (43' Olga PETROVA). (Coach: Igor SHALIMOV).

Referee: Dagmar DAMKOVÁ (CZE)   Attendance: 1,462.

Goals: 2' Ksenia TSYBUTOVICH 0-1, 22' Olesya KUROCHKINA 0-2, 24' Karen CARNEY 1-2, 31' Eniola ALUKO 2-2, 42' Kelly SMITH 3-2.

31.08.2009   Olympiastadion, Helsinki: Russia – Italy 0-2 (0-0).

RUSSIA: Elvira TODUA, Anna KOZHNIKOVA, Olga PORYADINA (60' Elena DANILOVA), Natalia PERTSEVA, Ksenia TSYBUTOVICH, Tatiana SKOTNIKOVA (46' Ekaterina SOCHNEVA), Valentina SAVCHENKOVA (68' Natalia BARBASHINA), Elena FOMINA, Elena MOROZOVA, Olesya KUROCHKINA, Olga PETROVA.
(Coach: Igor SHALIMOV).

ITALY: Anna PICARELLI, Sara GAMA, Roberta D'ADDA, Elisabetta TONA, Viviana SCHIAVI, Alessia TUTTINO (74' Tatiana ZORRI), Carolina PINI (64' Alia GUAGNI), Marta CARISSIMI, Giulia DOMENICHETTI, Melania GABBIADINI, Patrizia PANICO.
(Coach: Pietro GHEDIN).

Referee: Gyöngyi GAÁL (HUN)   Attendance: 1,112.

Goals: 77' Melania GABBIADINI 0-1, 90' Tatiana ZORRI 0-2.

Yellow Cards: Natalia PERTSEVA, Ksenia TSYBUTOVICH, Marta CARISSIMI.

31.08.2009   Veritas, Turku: Sweden – England 1-1 (1-1).

SWEDEN: Hedvig LINDAHL, Charlotte ROHLIN, Stina SEGERSTRÖM, Anna PAULSON, Sara THUNEBRO, Caroline SEGER, Kosovare ASLLANI (68' Lina NILSSON), Therese SJÖGRAN, Lisa DAHLKVIST (60' Jessica LANDSTRÖM), Lotta SCHELIN (90' Sara LINDÉN), Victoria SVENSSON.   (Coach: Thomas DENNERBY).

ENGLAND: Rachel BROWN-FINNIS, Alex SCOTT, Casey STONEY, Lindsay JOHNSON, Faye WHITE, Fara WILLIAMS, Katie CHAPMAN, Kelly SMITH, Karen CARNEY, Eniola ALUKO (65' Emily WESTWOOD), Sue SMITH (90' Jess CLARKE).
(Coach: Hope POWELL).

Referee: Kateryna MONZUL (UKR)   Attendance: 6,142.

Goals: 28' Faye WHITE 0-1, 40' Victoria SVENSSON 1-1 (p).

Yellow Cards: Kosovare ASLLANI, Therese SJÖGRAN.

FINAL STANDINGS

1.	SWEDEN	3	2	1	0	6	- 1	7
2.	ITALY	3	2	0	1	4	- 3	6
3.	ENGLAND	3	1	1	1	5	- 5	4
4.	RUSSIA	3	0	0	3	2	- 8	0

THIRD PLACE STANDINGS

1.	ENGLAND	3	1	1	1	5	-	5	4
2.	NORWAY	3	1	1	1	2	-	5	4
3.	DENMARK	3	1	0	2	3	-	4	3

England and Norway progressed to the Quarter-finals as the two third-placed teams with the best record.

QUARTER-FINALS

03.09.2009 Veritas, Turku: Finland – England 2-3 (0-1).

FINLAND: Tinja-Riikka KORPELA, Petra VAELMA, Tiina SALMÉN, Tuija HYYRYNEN, Maija SAARI, Jessica JULIN (72' Anna WESTELUND), Anne MÄKINEN, Essi SAINIO (52' Annica SJÖLUND), Laura KALMARI, Linda SÄLLSTROM, Sanna TALONEN (75' Susanna LEHTINEN). (Coach: Michael KÄLD).

ENGLAND: Rachel BROWN-FINNIS, Casey STONEY, Lindsay JOHNSON (68' Laura BASSETT), Faye WHITE (41' Jill SCOTT), Fara WILLIAMS, Anita ASANTE, Katie CHAPMAN, Kelly SMITH, Karen CARNEY, Eniola ALUKO, Sue SMITH. (Coach: Hope POWELL).

Referee: Dagmar DAMKOVÁ (CZE)   Attendance: 7,247.

Goals: 14' Eniola ALUKO 0-1, 49' Fara WILLIAMS 0-2, 65' Annica SJÖLUND 1-2, 67' Eniola ALUKO 1-3, 79' Linda SÄLLSTROM 2-3.

03.09.2009   Ratina, Tampere: Netherlands – France 0-0.

NETHERLANDS: Loes GEURTS, Dyanne BITO, Daphne KOSTER, Manoe MEULEN, Petra HOGEWONING, Anouk HOOGENDIJK, Annemieke KIESEL, Kirsten VAN DE VEN (77' Claudia VAN DEN HEILIGENBERG), Manon MELIS, Karin STEVENS, Sylvia SMIT. (Coach: Vera PAUW).

FRANCE: Céline DEVILLE, Ophélie MEILLEROUX, Laura GEORGES, Sandrine SOUBEYRAND, Corine PETIT, Sonia BOMPASTOR, Camille ABILY, Louisa CADAMURO (55' Eugénie LE SOMMER), Gaëtane THINEY (87' Candie HERBERT), Amandine HENRY, Élodie THOMIS. (Coach: Bruno BINI).

Referee: Kirsi HEIKKINEN (FIN)   Attendance: 2,766.

Yellow Card: Daphne KOSTER.

Netherlands won 5-4 on penalties.

Penalties: Sandrine SOUBEYRAND 0-1, Karin STEVENS 1-1, Camille ABILY 1-2, Manon MELIS 2-2, Amandine HENRY 2-3, Annemieke KIESEL 3-3, Eugénie LE SOMMER 3-4, Sylvia SMIT 4-4, Corine PETIT missed, Daphne KOSTER missed, Ophélie MEILLEROUX missed, Dyanne BITO missed, Candie HERBERT missed, Anouk HOOGENDIJK 5-4.

04.09.2009   Lahden, Lahti: Germany – Italy 2-1 (1-0).

GERMANY: Nadine ANGERER, Babett PETER, Annike KRAHN, Ariane HINGST (46' Sonja FUSS), Bianca SCHMIDT (46' Simone LAUDEHR), Melanie BEHRINGER, Linda BRESONIK, Kim KULIG-SOYAH, Kerstin GAREFREKES, Inka GRINGS, Birgit PRINZ (83' Martina MÜLLER). (Coach: Silvia NEID).

ITALY: Anna PICARELLI, Sara GAMA, Roberta D'ADDA, Elisabetta TONA, Viviana SCHIAVI, Alessia TUTTINO, Carolina PINI (88' Silvia FUSELLI), Marta CARISSIMI (82' Tatiana ZORRI), Giulia DOMENICHETTI, Melania GABBIADINI, Patrizia PANICO. (Coach: Pietro GHEDIN).

Referee: Jenny PALMQVIST (SWE)   Attendance: 1,866.

Goals: 4', 47' Inka GRINGS 1-0, 2-0, 63' Patrizia PANICO 2-1.

Yellow Card: Melania GABBIADINI.

04.09.2009   Finnair Stadium, Helsinki: Sweden – Norway 1-3 (0-2).

SWEDEN: Hedvig LINDAHL, Charlotte ROHLIN, Stina SEGERSTRÖM (67' Louise SCHILLGARD), Anna PAULSON, Sara THUNEBRO, Nilla FISCHER (46' Lina NILSSON), Caroline SEGER, Kosovare ASLLANI (46' Jessica LANDSTRÖM), Therese SJÖGRAN, Lotta SCHELIN, Victoria SVENSSON.   (Coach: Thomas DENNERBY).

NORWAY: Ingrid HJELMSETH, Toril AKERHAUGEN, Camilla HUSE, Maren MJELDE, Ingvidl STENSLAND, Anneli GISKE, Solveig GULBRANDSEN, Lene STORLØKKEN (90' Marita LUND), Trine BJERKE RØNNING, Isabell HERLOVSEN (76' Ingvild ISAKSEN), Elise THORSNES (57' Cecilie PEDERSEN).   (Coach: Bjarne BERNTSEN).

Referee: Bibiana STEINHAUS (GER)   Attendance: 1,708.

Goals: 39' Stina SEGERSTRÖM 0-1 (og), 44' Anneli GISKE 0-2, 60' Cecilie PEDERSEN 0-3, 80' Victoria SVENSSON 1-3.

Yellow Card: Therese SJÖGRAN.

SEMI-FINALS

06.09.2009   Ratina, Tampere: England – Netherlands 2-1 (0-0, 1-1).

ENGLAND: Rachel BROWN-FINNIS, Alex SCOTT, Casey STONEY, Lindsay JOHNSON, Fara WILLIAMS, Anita ASANTE, Katie CHAPMAN, Kelly SMITH, Jess CLARKE (91' Jill SCOTT), Eniola ALUKO (70' Lianne SANDERSON), Sue SMITH (46' Karen CARNEY). (Coach: Hope POWELL).

NETHERLANDS: Loes GEURTS, Dyanne BITO (117' Marloes DE BOER), Daphne KOSTER, Manoe MEULEN, Petra HOGEWONING, Anouk HOOGENDIJK, Annemieke KIESEL, Marlous PIEËTE (86' Kirsten VAN DE VEN), Manon MELIS, Karin STEVENS (120' Shanice VAN DE SANDEN), Sylvia SMIT.   (Coach: Vera PAUW).

Referee: Gyöngyi GAÁL (HUN)   Attendance: 4,621.

Goals: 61' Kelly SMITH 1-0, 64' Marlous PIEËTE 1-1, 116' Jill SCOTT 2-1.

Yellow Card: Casey STONEY.

England won following extra time.

07.09.2009   Finnair Stadium, Helsinki: Germany – Norway 3-1 (0-1).

GERMANY: Nadine ANGERER, Saskia BARTUSIAK, Babett PETER, Annike KRAHN, Bianca SCHMIDT (46' Célia ŠAŠIĆ), Melania BEHRINGER (60' Fatmire ALUSHI), Linda BRESONIK, Kim KULIG-SOYAH, Kerstin GAREFREKES, Inka GRINGS, Birgit PRINZ. (Coach: Silvia NEID).

NORWAY: Ingrid HJELMSETH, Toril AKERHAUGEN, Marita LUND, Camilla HUSE (82' Hedda STRAND GARDSJORD), Maren MJELDE, Ingvidl STENSLAND, Anneli GISKE, Solveig GULBRANDSEN (76' Melissa WIIK), Leni KAURIN (62' Cecilie PEDERSEN), Lene STORLØKKEN, Isabell HERLOVSEN. (Coach: Bjarne BERNTSEN).

Referee: Kirsi HEIKKINEN (FIN)   Attendance: 2,765.

Goals: 9' Isabell HERLOVSEN 0-1, 59' Simone LAUDEHR 1-1, 61' Célia ŠAŠIĆ 2-1, 90' Fatmire ALUSHI 3-1.

Yellow Cards: Toril AKERHAUGEN, Maren MJELDE.

FINAL

10.09.2009   Olympiastadion, Helsinki: England – Germany 2-6 (1-2).

ENGLAND: Rachel BROWN-FINNIS, Alex SCOTT, Casey STONEY, Faye WHITE, Fara WILLIAMS, Anita ASANTE, Katie CHAPMAN (86' Emily WESTWOOD), Kelly SMITH, Jill SCOTT, Karen CARNEY, Eniola ALUKO (81' Lianne SANDERSON). (Coach: Hope POWELL).

GERMANY: Nadine ANGERER, Saskia BARTUSIAK, Babett PETER, Annike KRAHN, Simone LAUDEHR, Melania BEHRINGER (60' Célia ŠAŠIĆ), Linda BRESONIK, Kim KULIG-SOYAH, Kerstin GAREFREKES (83' Fatmire ALUSHI), Inka GRINGS, Birgit PRINZ. (Coach: Silvia NEID).

Referee: Dagmar DAMKOVÁ (CZE)   Attendance: 15,877.

Goals: 20' Birgit PRINZ 0-1, 23' Melania BEHRINGER 0-2, 24' Karen CARNEY 1-2, 50' Kim KULIG-SOYAH 1-3, 55' Kelly SMITH 2-3, 62', 73' Inka GRINGS 2-4, 2-5, 76' Birgit PRINZ 2-6.

Yellow Card: Casey STONEY.

Germany were European Champions

UEFA EUROPEAN WOMEN'S CHAMPIONSHIP
EURO 2013

The fomat was the same as the previous tournament in 2009. The number 1 and 2 of each group, together with the 2 best number 3 countries proceed to the quarter-finals. All matches were played in Sweden.

GROUP A

10.07.2013   Örjans Vall, Halmstad: Italy – Finland 0-0.

ITALY:: Chiara MARCHITELLI, Roberta D'ADDA, Elisa BARTOLI, Raffaella MANIERI, Cecilia SALVAI, Alessia TUTTINO, Alice PARISI, Elisa CAMPORESE (70' Sandy IANNELLA), Daniela STRACCHI, Melania GABBIADINI, Patrizia PANICO. (Coach: Antonio CABRINI).

FINLAND: Tinja-RIIKKA KORPELA, Tuija HYYRYNEN, Susanna LEHTINEN, Laura KIVISTÖ, Annika KUKKONEN, Emmi ALANEN, Nora HEROUM, Anna WESTERLUND, Marianna TOLVANEN (73' Natalia KUIKKA), Sanna TALONEN, Annica SJÖLUND (61' Jaana LYYTIKÄINEN).   (Coach: Andrée JEGLERTZ).

Referee: Teodora ALBON (ROM)   Attendance: 3,011.

Yellow Cards: Elisa CAMPORESE, Emmi ALANEN, Anna WESTERLUND, Jaana LYYTIKÄINEN.

10.07.2013   Gamla Ullevi, Göteborg: Sweden – Denmark 1-1 (1-1).

SWEDEN: Kristin HAMMARSTRÖM, Charlotte ROHLIN, Nilla FISCHER, Sara THUNEBRO, Jessica SAMUELSSON, Antonia GÖRANSSON (63' Lisa DAHLKVIST), Caroline SEGER, Marie HAMMARSTRÖM, Lotta SCHELIN, Kosovare ASLLANI, Josefine ÖQVIST (79' Sofia JAKOBSSON).   (Coach: Pia SUNDHAGE).

DENMARK: Stina PETERSEN, Line RØDDIK, Christina ØRNTOFT, Mariann KNUDSEN, Theresa NIELSEN, Mia BROGAARD, Katrine SØNDERGAARD PEDERSEN, Sofie PEDERSEN (46' Nadia NADIM), Pernille HARDER, Katrine VEJE (62' Julie RYDAHL), Johanna RASMUSSEN (898' Line JENSEN).   (Coach: Kenneth HEINER-MØLLER).

Referee: Bibiana STEINHAUS (GER)   Attendance: 16,128.

Goals: 26' Mariann KNUDSEN 0-1, 35' Nilla FISCHER 1-1.

Yellow Cards: Christina ØRNTOFT, Theresa NIELSEN.

Lotta Schelin missed a penalty in the 67st minute and Kosovare Asllani missed a penalty in the 85st minute.

13.07.2013   Örjans Vall, Halmstad: Italy – Denmark 2-1 (0-0).

ITALY: Chiara MARCHITELLI, Roberta D'ADDA, Elisa BARTOLI, Raffaella MANIERI, Cecilia SALVAI, Alessia TUTTINO, Alice PARISI (58' Ilaria MAURO), Sandy IANNELLA (86' Giulia DOMENICHETTI), Daniela STRACCHI, Melania GABBIADINI, Patrizia PANICO (71' Martina ROSUCCI).   (Coach: Antonio CABRINI).

DENMARK: Stina PETERSEN, Line RØDDIK, Christina ØRNTOFT, Mariann KNUDSEN, Theresa NIELSEN (86' Emma MADSEN), Mia BROGAARD, Katrine SØNDERGAARD PEDERSEN, Sofie PEDERSEN (46' Nadia NADIM), Pernille HARDER, Katrine VEJE (65' Julie RYDAHL), Johanna RASMUSSEN.   (Coach: Kenneth HEINER-MØLLER).

Referee: Esther STAUBLI (SUI)   Attendance: 2,190.

Goals: 55' Melania GABBIADINI 1-0, 60' ILARIA MAURO 2-0, 66' Mia BROGAARD 2-1.

Yellow Cards: Elisa BARTOLI, Raffaella MANIERI, Alessia TUTTINO.

13.07.2013   Gamla Ullevi, Göteborg: Finland – Sweden 0-5 (0-3).

FINLAND: Tinja-RIIKKA KORPELA, Tuija HYYRYNEN, Susanna LEHTINEN, Laura KIVISTÖ, Annika KUKKONEN, Emmi ALANEN, Nora HEROUM, Anna WESTERLUND, Jaana LYYTIKÄINEN (87' Natalia KUIKKA), Marianna TOLVANEN (31' Tiina SAARIO), Sanna TALONEN (69' Ella VANHANEN).   (Coach: Andrée JEGLERTZ).

SWEDEN: Kristin HAMMARSTRÖM, Charlotte ROHLIN, Nilla FISCHER, Sara THUNEBRO, Lina NILSSON, Caroline SEGER, Marie HAMMARSTRÖM (56' Lisa DAHLKVIST), Lotta SCHELIN, Kosovare ASLLANI (72' Jenny HJOHLMAN), Sofia JAKOBSSON, Josefine ÖQVIST (67' Antonia GÖRANSSON).   (Coach: Pia SUNDHAGE).

Referee: Cristina DORCIOMAN (ROM)   Attendance: 16,414.

Goals: 15', 36' Nilla FISCHER 0-1, 0-2, 38' Kosovare ASSLANI 0-3, 60', 87' Lotta SCHELIN 0-4, 0-5.

16.07.2013   Örjans Vall, Halmstad: Sweden – Italy 3-1 (0-0).

SWEDEN: Kristin HAMMARSTRÖM, Charlotte ROHLIN, Nilla FISCHER, Sara THUNEBRO (79' Olivia SCHOUGH), Jessica SAMUELSSON, Lisa DAHLKVIST, Caroline SEGER (64' Lina NILSSON), Marie HAMMARSTRÖM, Lotta SCHELIN, Kosovare ASLLANI (46' Therese SJÖGRAN), Josefine ÖQVIST. (Coach: Pia SUNDHAGE).

ITALY: Chiara MARCHITELLI, Sara GAMA, Roberta D'ADDA, Raffaella MANIERI, Giorgia MOTTA, Cristiana GIRELLI (52' Giulia DOMENICHETTI), Alice PARISI, Sandy IANNELLA, Martina ROSUCCI, Ilaria MAURO (62' Patrizia PANICO), Paola BRUMANA (63' Melania GABBIADINI). (Coach: Antonio CABRINI).

Referee: Katalin KULCSÁR (HUN)   Attendance: 7,288.

Goals: 47' Raffaella MANIERI 1-0 (og), 49' Lotta SCHELIN 2-0, 57' Josefine ÖQVIST 3-0, 78' Melania GABBIADINI 3-1.

Yellow Cards: Nilla FISCHER, Giorgia MOTTA, Martina ROSUCCI.

16.07.2013   Gamla Ullevi, Göteborg: Denmark – Finland 1-1 (1-0).

DENMARK: Stina PETERSEN, Line RØDDIK, Christina ØRNTOFT, Mariann KNUDSEN, Theresa NIELSEN, Mia BROGAARD, Cecilie SANDVEJ, Katrine SØNDERGAARD PEDERSEN, Julie RYDAHL (64' Nanna CHRISTIANSEN), Pernille HARDER (84' Karoline SMIDT), Nadia NADIM (64' Johanna RASMUSSEN).
(Coach: Kenneth HEINER-MØLLER).

FINLAND: Minna MERILUOTO, Tuija HYYRYNEN, Susanna LEHTINEN (46' Natalia KUIKKA), Laura KIVISTÖ (79' Heidi KIVELÄ), Tiina SAARIO, Annika KUKKONEN, Katri NOKSO-KOIVISTO, Emmi ALANEN, Nora HEROUM (69' Sanna TALONEN), Anna WESTERLUND, Annica SJÖLUND. (Coach: Andrée JEGLERTZ).

Referee: Kateryna MONZUL (UKR)   Attendance: 8,360.

Goals: 28' Mia BROGAARD 1-0, 87' Annica SJÖLUND 1-1.

Yellow Cards: Cecilie SANDVEJ, Annika KUKKONEN.

FINAL STANDINGS

1.	SWEDEN	3	2	1	0	9	-	2	7
2.	ITALY	3	1	1	1	3	-	4	4
3.	DENMARK	3	0	2	1	3	-	4	2
4.	FINLAND	3	0	2	1	1	-	6	2

GROUP B

11.07.2013   Guldfågeln Arena, Kalmar: Norway – Iceland 1-1 (1-0).

NORWAY: Ingrid HJELMSETH, Marit CHRISTENSEN, Toril AKERHAUGEN, Maren MJELDE, Ingvild STENSLAND (75' Lene MYKJÅLAND), Trine BJERKE RØNNING, Solveig GULBRANDSEN, Caroline GRAHAM HANSEN (85' Leni KAURIN), Kristine HEGLAND-MINDE, Ingvild ISAKSEN, Ada STOLSMO HEGERBERG (75' Elise THORSNES). (Coach: Even PELLERUD).

ICELAND: Gudbjörg GUNNARSDÓTTIR, Sif ATLADÓTTIR (63' Glódis VIGGÓSDÓTTIR), Katrin JÓNSDÓTTIR, Hallbera GISLADÓTTIR, Hólmfridur MAGNÚSDÓTTIR, Sara Björk GUNNARSDÓTTIR, Margrét Lára VIDARSDÓTTIR, Dóra Maria LÁRUSDÓTTIR, Dagný BRYNJARSDÓTTIR (83' Katrin OMARSDÓTTIR), Fanndis FRIDRIKSDÓTTIR (63' Harpa PORSTEINSDÓTTIR), Rakel HÖNNUDÓTTIR. (Coach: Sigurdur EYJÓLFSSON).

Referee: Katalin KULCSÁR (HUN)   Attendance: 3,867.

Goals: 26' Kristine HEGLAND-MINDE 1-0, 87' Margrét Lára VIDARSDÓTTIR 1-1 (p).

Yellow Cards: Marit CHRISTENSEN, Hólmfridur MAGNÚSDÓTTIR.

11.07.2013   Myresjöhus Arena, Växjö: Germany – Netherlands 0-0.

GERMANY: Nadine ANGERER, Saskia BARTUSIAK, Leonie MAIER, Annike KRAHN, Jennifer CRAMER, Nadine KESSLER (46' Simone LAUDEHR), Lena GOESSLING, Lena LOTZEN (73' Melanie LEUPOLZ), Dzsenifer MAROZSÁN, Anja MITTAG, Célia ŠAŠIĆ. (Coach: Silvia NEID).
NETHERLANDS: Loes GEURTS, Dyanne BITO, Daphne KOSTER, Anouk HOOGENDIJK, Sherida SPITSE, Daniëlle VAN DE DONK, Claudia VAN DEN HEILIGENBERG, Kirsten VAN DE VEN, Manon MELIS, Lieke MARTENS, Renée SLEGERS. (Coach: Roger REIJNERS).

Referee: Silvia SPINELLI (ITA)   Attendance: 8,861.

Yellow Cards: Leonie MAIER, Jennifer CRAMER, Nadine KESSLER, Dyanne BITO.

14.07.2013   Guldfågeln Arena, Kalmar: Norway – Netherlands 1-0 (0-0).

NORWAY: Ingrid HJELMSETH, Marit CHRISTENSEN, Toril AKERHAUGEN, Maren MJELDE, Ingvild STENSLAND, Trine BJERKE RØNNING, Solveig GULBRANDSEN (72' Cathrine HØGH DEKKERHUS), Caroline GRAHAM HANSEN (79' Elise THORSNES), Kristine HEGLAND-MINDE, Ingvild ISAKSEN, Ada STOLSMO HEGERBERG (72' Melissa BJÅNESØY). (Coach: Even PELLERUD).

NETHERLANDS: Loes GEURTS, Dyanne BITO, Daphne KOSTER, Anouk HOOGENDIJK, Sherida SPITSE (85' Anouk DEKKER), Daniëlle VAN DE DONK (77' Mandy VERSTEEGT), Claudia VAN DEN HEILIGENBERG (60' Siri WORM), Kirsten VAN DE VEN, Manon MELIS, Lieke MARTENS, Renée SLEGERS. (Coach: Roger REIJNERS).

Referee: Teodora ALBON (ROM)   Attendance: 4,256.

Goal: 54' Solveig GULBRANDSEN 1-0.

14.07.2013   Myresjöhus Arena, Växjö: Iceland – Germany 0-3 (0-1).

ICELAND: Gudbjörg GUNNARSDÓTTIR, Glódis VIGGÓSDÓTTIR, Katrin JÓNSDÓTTIR, Hallbera GISLADÓTTIR, Hólmfridur MAGNÚSDÓTTIR, Sara Björk GUNNARSDÓTTIR (60' Olina VIDARSDÓTTIR), Margrét Lára VIDARSDÓTTIR, Dóra Maria LÁRUSDÓTTIR, Dagný BRYNJARSDÓTTIR (46' Katrin OMARSDÓTTIR / 70' Gudný Björk ODINSDÓTTIR), Harpa PORSTEINSDÓTTIR, Rakel HÖNNUDÓTTIR. (Coach: Sigurdur EYJÓLFSSON).

GERMANY: Nadine ANGERER, Saskia BARTUSIAK, Leonie MAIER, Annike KRAHN, Jennifer CRAMER, Nadine KESSLER, Melanie LEUPOLZ, Lena GOESSLING (70' Simone LAUDEHR), Lena LOTZEN (64' Fatmire ALUSHI), Dzsenifer MAROZSÁN (74' Anja MITTAG), Célia ŠAŠIĆ. (Coach: Silvia NEID).

Referee: Kirsi HEIKKINEN (FIN)   Attendance: 4,620.

Goals: 24' Lena LOTZEN 0-1, 55', 84' Célia ŠAŠIĆ 0-2, 0-3.

Yellow Cards: Katrin JÓNSDÓTTIR, Jennifer CRAMER.

17.07.2013   Myresjöhus Arena, Växjö: Netherlands – Iceland 0-1 (0-1).

NETHERLANDS: Loes GEURTS, Dyanne BITO, Daphne KOSTER, Anouk HOOGENDIJK, Sherida SPITSE, Daniëlle VAN DE DONK, Claudia VAN DEN HEILIGENBERG, Kirsten VAN DE VEN (77' Sylvia SMIT), Manon MELIS, Lieke MARTENS, Renée SLEGERS (46' Anouk DEKKER). (Coach: Roger REIJNERS).

ICELAND: Gudbjörg GUNNARSDÓTTIR, Sif ATLADÓTTIR, Katrin JÓNSDÓTTIR, Hallbera GISLADÓTTIR, Hólmfridur MAGNÚSDÓTTIR, Sara Björk GUNNARSDÓTTIR, Margrrét Lára VIDARSDÓTTIR (62' Harpa PORSTEINSDÓTTIR), Dóra Maria LÁRUSDÓTTIR, Dagný BRYNJARSDÓTTIR, Fanndis FRIDRIKSDÓTTIR (86' Olina VIDARSDÓTTIR), Rakel HÖNNUDÓTTIR. (Coach: Sigurdur EYJÓLFSSON).

Referee: Cristina DORCIOMAN (ROM)   Attendance: 3,406.

Goal: 30' Dagný BRYNJARSDÓTTIR 0-1.

Yellow Cards: Daphne KOSTER, Renée SLEGERS, Hólmfridur MAGNÚSDÓTTIR.

17.07.2013   Guldfågeln Arena, Kalmar: Germany – Norway 0-1 (0-1).

GERMANY: Nadine ANGERER, Saskia BARTUSIAK, Leonie MAIER, Annike KRAHN, Luisa WENSING, Simone LAUDEHR (67' Melanie BEHRINGER), Nadine KESSLER, Melanie LEUPOLZ (67' Anja MITTAG), Lena LOTZEN (80' Sara DÄBRITZ), Dzsenifer MAROZSÁN, Célia ŠAŠIĆ. (Coach: Silvia NEID).

NORWAY: Ingrid HJELMSETH, Marita LUND, Toril AKERHAUGEN, Maren MJELDE, Nora HOLSTAD BERGE, Gry TOFTE IMS (58' Solveig GULBRANDSEN), Cathrine HØGH DEKKERHUS, Elise THORSNES (58' Caroline GRAHAM HANSEN), Ingvild ISAKSEN, Emilie HAAVI (72' Ingvild STENSLAND), Ada STOLSMO HEGERBERG. (Coach: Even PELLERUD).

Referee: Esther STAUBLI (SUI)   Attendance: 10,346.

Goal: 45' Ingvild ISAKSEN 0-1.

Yellow Card: Gry TOFTE IMS.

FINAL STANDINGS

1.	NORWAY	3	2	1	0	3	-	1	7
2.	GERMANY	3	1	1	1	3	-	1	4
3.	ICELAND	3	1	1	1	2	-	4	4
4.	NETHERLANDS	3	0	1	2	0	-	2	1

GROUP C

12.07.2013   Nya Parken, Norrköping: France – Russia 3-1 (2-0).

FRANCE: Sarah BOUHADDI, Wendie RENARD, Laure BOULLEAU, Laura GEORGES, Sandrine SOUBEYRAND (76' Camille CATALA), Corine PETIT, Élise BUSSAGLIA, Gaëtane THINEY (66' Louisa CADAMURO), Camille ABILY, Eugénie LE SOMMER, Marie-Laure DELIE (61' Élodie THOMAS).   (Coach: Bruno BINI).

RUSSIA: Elvira TODUA, Valentina SAVCHENKOVA (35' Anastasia POZDEEVA / 68' Tatiana SKOTNIKOVA), Anastasia KOSTYUKOVA, Elena MEDVED (35' Yulia GORDEEVA), Ksenia TSYBUTOVICH, Olga PETROVA, Elena TEREKHOVA, Alla SIDOROVSKAYA, Elena MOROZOVA, Ekaterina SOCHNEVA, Nelli KOROVKINA. (Coach: Sergei LAVRENTYEV).

Referee: Jenny PALMQVIST (SWE)   Attendance: 2,980.

Goals: 21', 32' Marie-Laure DELIE 1-0, 2-0, 67' Eugénie LE SOMMER 3-0, 84' Elena MOROZOVA 3-1.

Yellow Cards: Anastasia KOSTYUKOVA, Tatiana SKOTNIKOVA.

12.07.2013   Linköping Arena, Linköping: England – Spain 2-3 (1-1).

ENGLAND: Karen BARDSLEY, Alex SCOTT, Steph HOUGHTON, Casey STONEY, Laura BASSETT, Jill SCOTT, Anita ASANTE, Fara WILLIAMS, Rachel YANKEY (90' Jess CLARKE), Eniola ALUKO (72' Karen CARNEY), Ellen WHITE.   (Coach: Hope POWELL).

SPAIN: AINHOA Tirapu de Goñi, RUTH Garcia Garcia, Marta TORREJÓN Moya, IRENE Paredes Hernández, Silvia MESEGUER Bellido, Elisabeth IBARRA Raboncha, Jenni HERMOSO Fuentes, SONIA Bermúdez Tribano (74' ALEXIA Putellas Segura), Verónica BOQUETE Giadans, Adriana MARTIN Santamaria, Nagore CALDERÓN Rodriguez (61' Maria Victoria LOSADA Gómez).   (Coach: Ignacio QUEREDA).

Referee: Kateryna MONZUL (UKR)   Attendance: 5,190.

Goals: 4' Verónica BOQUETE Giadans 0-1, 8' Eniola Aluko 1-1, Jenni HERMOSO Fuentes 1-2, 89' Laura BASSETT 2-2, 90' ALEXIA Putellas Segura 2-3.

Yellow Cards: Laura BASSETT, IRENE Paredes Hernández, Nagore CALDERÓN Rodriguez.

15.07.2013 Linköping Arena, Linköping: England – Russia 1-1 (0-1).

ENGLAND: Karen BARDSLEY, Alex SCOTT, Steph HOUGHTON (64' Toni DUGGAN), Casey STONEY, Laura BASSETT, Jill SCOTT, Anita ASANTE, Fara WILLIAMS, Rachel YANKEY (17' Karen CARNEY), Eniola ALUKO (78' Kelly SMITH), Ellen WHITE. (Coach: Hope POWELL).

RUSSIA: Elvira TODUA, Valentina SAVCHENKOVA (84' Maria DYACHKOVA), Anastasia KOSTYUKOVA, Elena MEDVED, Ksenia TSYBUTOVICH, Olga PETROVA, Elena TEREKHOVA (90' Olesya KUROCHKINA), Alla SIDOROVSKAYA, Elena MOROZOVA, Ekaterina SOCHNEVA, Nelli KOROVKINA (90' Natalia SHLYAPINA). (Coach: Sergei LAVRENTYEV).

Referee: Bibiana STEINHAUS (GER) Attendance: 3,629.

Goals: 38' Nelli KOROVKINA 0-1, 90' Toni DUGGAN 1-1.

Yellow Cards: Fara WILLIAMS, Kelly SMITH.

15.07.2013 Nya Parken, Norrköping: Spain – France 0-1 (0-1).

SPAIN: AINHOA Tirapu de Goñi, Marta TORREJÓN Moya, IRENE Paredes Hernández, MIRIAM Diéguez de Oña, SANDRA Vilanova Tous (85' ERIKA Vázquez Morales), Silvia MESEGUER Bellido, Elisabeth IBARRA Raboncha, Jenni HERMOSO Fuentes, SONIA Bermúdez Tribano (78' ALEXIA Putellas Segura), Verónica BOQUETE Giadans, Adriana MARTIN Santamaria (78' Maria Victoria LOSADA Gómez). (Coach: Ignacio QUEREDA).

FRANCE: Sarah BOUHADDI, Wendie RENARD, Laure BOULLEAU, Laura GEORGES, Sandrine SOUBEYRAND (46' Élodie THOMAS), Corine PETIT, Élise BUSSAGLIA, Louisa CADAMURO (63' Eugénie LE SOMMER) Gaëtane THINEY, Camille ABILY, Marie-Laure DELIE. (Coach: Bruno BINI).

Referee: Carina VITULANO (ITA) Attendance: 5,068.

Goal: 5' Wendie RENARD 0-1.

18.07.2013　　　Nya Parken, Norrköping: Russia – Spain 1-1 (1-1).

RUSSIA: Elvira TODUA, Valentina SAVCHENKOVA, Anastasia KOSTYUKOVA (34' Daria MAKARENKO), Elena MEDVED, Ksenia TSYBUTOVICH, Olga PETROVA, Elena TEREKHOVA, Alla SIDOROVSKAYA, Elena MOROZOVA, Ekaterina SOCHNEVA (58' Yulia BESSOLOVA), Nelli KOROVKINA. (Coach: Sergei LAVRENTYEV).

SPAIN: AINHOA Tirapu de Goñi, RUTH Garcia Garcia, Marta TORREJÓN Moya, IRENE Paredes Hernández, ALEXIA Putellas Segura (68' SONIA Bermúdez Tribano), Maria Victoria LOSADA Gómez (64' NAGORE CALDERÓN Rodriguez), Silvia MESEGUER Bellido, Elisabeth IBARRA Raboncha, Jenni HERMOSO Fuentes, Verónica BOQUETE Giadans, Adriana MARTIN Santamaria. (Coach: Ignacio QUEREDA).

Referee: Jenny PALMQVIST (SWE)　　Attendance: 7,332.

Goals: 14' Verónica BOQUETE Giadans 0-1, 44' Elena TEREKHOVA 1-1.

Yellow Cards: Elena MEDVED, Nelli KOROVKINA.

18.07.2013　　　Linköping Arena, Linköping: France – England 3-0 (1-0).

FRANCE: Céline DEVILLE, Wendie RENARD, Sandrine SOUBEYRAND (46' Élise BUSSAGLIA), Corine PETIT, Sabrine DELANNOY, Amandine HENRY (61' Camille CATALA), Louisa CADAMURO, Jessica HOUARA D'HOMMEAUX, Gaëtane THINEY (46' Camille ABILY, Eugénie LE SOMMER, Élodie THOMIS. (Coach: Bruno BINI).

ENGLAND: Karen BARDSLEY, Alex SCOTT, Steph HOUGHTON, Sophie BRADLEY, Casey STONEY, Anita ASANTE (46' Jill SCOTT), Fara WILLIAMS, Karen CARNEY (73' Jess CLARKE), Eniola ALUKO (60' Kelly SMITH), Ellen WHITE, Toni DUGGAN. (Coach: Hope POWELL).

Referee: Kirsi HEIKKINEN (FIN)　　Attendance: 2,157.

Goals: 9' Eugénie LE SOMMER 1-0, 62' Louisa CADAMURO 2-0, 64' Wendie RENARD 3-0.

Yellow Card: Fara WILLIAMS.

FINAL STANDINGS

1.	FRANCE	3	3	0	0	7	-	1	9
2.	SPAIN	3	1	1	1	4	-	4	4
3.	RUSSIA	3	0	2	1	3	-	5	2
4.	ENGLAND	3	0	1	2	3	-	7	1

THIRD-PLACE STANDINGS

1.	ICELAND	3	1	1	1	2 - 4	4
2.	DENMARK	3	0	2	1	3 - 4	2
3.	RUSSIA	3	0	2	1	3 - 5	2

Iceland and Denmark progressed to the Quarter-finals as the two third-placed teams with the best record.

QUARTER-FINALS

21.07.2013   Örjans Vall, Halmstad: Sweden – Iceland 4-0 (3-0).

SWEDEN: Kristin HAMMARSTRÖM, Charlotte ROHLIN, Nilla FISCHER, Sara THUNEBRO, Jessica SAMUELSSON, Caroline SEGER, Marie HAMMARSTRÖM (63' Lisa DAHLKVIST), Lotta SCHELIN (67' Emmelie KONRADSSON), Kosovare ASLLANI, Sofia JAKOBSSON, Josefine ÖQVIST. (Coach: Pia SUNDHAGE).

ICELAND: Gudbjörg GUNNARSDÓTTIR, Sif ATLADÓTTIR, Olina VIDARSDÓTTIR, Katrin JÓNSDÓTTIR (80' Glódis VIGGÓSDÓTTIR), Hallbera GISLADÓTTIR, Sara Björk GUNNARSDÓTTIR, Margrrét Lára VIDARSDÓTTIR (78' Elin Metta JENSEN), Dóra Maria LÁRUSDÓTTIR, Dagný BRYNJARSDÓTTIR, Fanndis FRIDRIKSDÓTTIR (65' Harpa PORSTEINSDÓTTIR), Rakel HÖNNUDÓTTIR. (Coach: Sigurdur EYJÓLFSSON).

Referee: Kirsi HEIKKINEN (FIN)   Attendance: 7,468.

Goals: 3' Marie HAMMARSTRÖM 1-0, 14' Josefine ÖQVIST 2-0, 19', 59' Lotta SCHELIN 3-0, 4-0.

Yellow Card: Fanndis FRIDRIKSDÓTTIR.

21.07.2013   Myresjöhus Arena, Växjö: Italy – Germany 0-1 (0-1).

ITALY: Chiara MARCHITELLI, Roberta D'ADDA, Elisa BARTOLI, Raffaella MANIERI, Cecilia SALVAI (70' Federica DI CRISCIO), Alessia TUTTINO, Alice PARISI (75' Ilaria MAURO), Elisa CAMPORESE (46' Sandy IANNELLA), Daniela STRACCHI, Melania GABBIADINI, Patrizia PANICO. (Coach: Antonio CABRINI).

GERMANY: Nadine ANGERER, Saskia BARTUSIAK, Leonie MAIER, Annike KRAHN, Jennifer CRAMER, Simone LAUDEHR, Nadine KESSLER, Lena GOESSLING, Lena LOTZEN, Anja MITTAG (52' Dzsenifer MAROZSÁN), Célia ŠAŠIĆ (68' Sara DÄBRITZ). (Coach: Silvia NEID).

Referee: Katalin KULCSÁR (HUN)   Attendance: 9,265.

Goal: 26' Simone LAUDEHR 0-1.

Yellow Cards: Cecilia SALVAI, Alessia TUTTINO, Alice PARISI, Daniela STRACCHI, Federica DI CRISCIO.

22.07.2013   Guldfågeln Arena, Kalmar: Norway – Spain 3-1 (2-0).

NORWAY: Ingrid HJELMSETH, Marit CHRISTENSEN, Toril AKERHAUGEN, Maren MJELDE, Ingvild STENSLAND, Trine BJERKE RØNNING, Solveig GULBRANDSEN, Caroline GRAHAM HANSEN (81' Ingrid RYLAND), Kristine HEGLAND-MINDE, Ingvild ISAKSEN (77' Cathrine HØGH DEKKERHUS), Ada STOLSMO HEGERBERG (72' Elise THORSNES. (Coach: Even PELLERUD).

SPAIN: AINHOA Tirapu de Goñi, RUTH Garcia Garcia (63' ERIKA Vázquez Morales), Marta TORREJÓN Moya, IRENE Paredes Hernández, ALEXIA Putellas Segura, Silvia MESEGUER Bellido), Elisabeth IBARRA Raboncha (70' LEIRE Landa Iroz), Jenni HERMOSO Fuentes, Verónica BOQUETE Giadans, Adriana MARTIN Santamaria (77' Priscila BORJA Moreno), NAGORE CALDERÓN Rodriguez.   (Coach: Ignacio QUEREDA).

Referee: Bibiana STEINHAUS (GER)   Attendance: 10,435.

Goals: 24' Solveig GULBRANDSEN 1-0, 43' IRENE Paredes Hernández 2-0 (og), 64' Ada STOLSMO HEGERBERG 3-0, 90' Jenni HERMOSO Fuentes 3-1.

Yellow Card: LEIRE Landa Iroz.

22.07.2013   Linköping Arena, Linköping: France – Denmark 1-1 (0-1, 1-1, 1-1).

FRANCE: Sarah BOUHADDI, Wendie RENARD, Laure BOULLEAU, Laura GEORGES (58' Sabrina DELANNOY), Sandrine SOUBEYRAND (46' Élodie THOMAS), Corine PETIT, Élise BUSSAGLIA, Louisa CADAMURO, Gaëtane THINEY, Camille ABILY, Eugénie LE SOMMER. (Coach: Bruno BINI).

DENMARK: Stina PETERSEN, Line RØDDIK, Christina ØRNTOFT, Janni ARNTH, Mariann KNUDSEN, Theresa NIELSEN, Mia BROGAARD (75' Line JENSEN), Katrine SØNDERGAARD PEDERSEN, Pernille HARDER, Katrine VEJE (68' Nadia NADIM), Johanna RASMUSSEN (61' Julie RYDAHL). (Coach: Kenneth HEINER-MØLLER).

Referee: Carina VITULANO (ITA)   Attendance: 7,448.

Goals: 28' Johanna RASMUSSEN 0-1, 71' Louisa CADAMURO 1-1 (p).

Yellow Cards: Wendie RENARD, Janni ARNTH.

Denmark won 4-2 on penalties.

Penalties: Line RØDDIK 0-1, Louisa CADAMURO missed, Julie RYDAHL 0-2, Gaëtane THINEY 1-2, Nadia NADIM 1-3, Eugénie LE SOMMER 2-3, Theresa NIELSEN missed, Sandrine DELANNOY missed, Janni ARNTH 2-4.

SEMI-FINALS

24.07.2013   Gamla Ullevi, Göteborg: Sweden – Germay 0-1 (0-1).

SWEDEN: Kristin HAMMARSTRÖM, Charlotte ROHLIN, Nilla FISCHER, Sara THUNEBRO, Jessica SAMUELSSON (82' Lisa DAHLKVIST), Antonia GÖRANSSON (65' Therese SJÖGRAN), Caroline SEGER, Marie HAMMARSTRÖM, Lotta SCHELIN, Kosovare ASLLANI, Josefine ÖQVIST (74' Sofia JAKOBSSON). (Coach: Pia SUNDHAGE).

GERMANY: Nadine ANGERER, Saskia BARTUSIAK, Leonie MAIER, Annike KRAHN, Jennifer CRAMER, Simone LAUDEHR, Nadine KESSLER, Lena GOESSLING, Lena LOTZEN (78' Melanie LEUPOLZ), Dzsenifer MAROZSÁN (89' Bianca SCHMIDT), Anja MITTAG.   (Coach: Silvia NEID).

Referee: Esther STAUBLI (SUI)   Attendance: 16,628.

Goal: 33' Dzsenifer MAROZSÁN 0-1.

Yellow Cards: Nilla FISCHER, Simone LAUDEHR.

25.07.2013   Nya Parken, Norrköping: Norway – Denmark 1-1 (1-0, 1-1, 1-1).

NORWAY: Ingrid HJELMSETH, Marit CHRISTENSEN, Toril AKERHAUGEN, Maren MJELDE, Ingvild STENSLAND, Trine BJERKE RØNNING, Solveig GULBRANDSEN, Caroline GRAHAM HANSEN (58' Elise THORSNES), Kristine HEGLAND-MINDE, Ingvild ISAKSEN (63' Cathrine HØGH DEKKERHUS), Ada STOLSMO HEGERBERG (80' Emilie HAAVI). (Coach: Even PELLERUD).

DENMARK: Stina PETERSEN, Line RØDDIK, Christina ØRNTOFT (82' Emma MADSEN), Janni ARNTH (68' Johanna RASMUSSEN), Mariann KNUDSEN, Theresa NIELSEN, Mia BROGAARD, Katrine SØNDERGAARD PEDERSEN, Julie RYDAHL (68' Nadia NADIM), Pernille HARDER, Katrine VEJE. (Coach: Kenneth HEINER-MØLLER).

Referee: Kateryna MONZUL (UKR)   Attendance: 9,260.

Goals: 3' Marit CHRISTENSEN 1-0, 87' Mariann KNUDSEN 1-1.

Norway won 4-2 on penalties.

Penalties: Line RØDDIK missed, Solveig GULBRANDSEN 1-0, Theresa NIELSEN missed, Cathrine HØGH DEKKERHUS 2-0, Nadia NADIM 2-1, Maren MJELDE 3-1, Mia BROGAARD 3-2, Trine BJERKE RØNNING 4-2.

FINAL

28.07.2013   Friends Arena, Solna: Germany – Norway 1-0 (0-0).

GERMANY: Nadine ANGERER, Saskia BARTUSIAK, Leonie MAIER, Annike KRAHN, Jennifer CRAMER, Simone LAUDEHR, Nadine KESSLER, Lena GOESSLING, Lena LOTZEN (78' Melanie LEUPOLZ), Dzsenifer MAROZSÁN (89' Bianca SCHMIDT), Anja MITTAG. (Coach: Silvia NEID).

NORWAY: Ingrid HJELMSETH, Marit CHRISTENSEN, Toril AKERHAUGEN, Maren MJELDE, Ingvild STENSLAND, Trine BJERKE RØNNING, Solveig GULBRANDSEN, Caroline GRAHAM HANSEN (58' Elise THORSNES), Kristine HEGLAND-MINDE, Ingvild ISAKSEN (63' Cathrine HØGH DEKKERHUS), Ada STOLSMO HEGERBERG (80' Emilie HAAVI). (Coach: Even PELLERUD).

Referee: Cristina Dorcioman (ROM)   Attendance: 41,301.

Goal: 49' Anja MITTAG 1-0.

Yellow Card: Annike KRAHN.

Trine Bjerke Rønning missed a penalty in the 29th minute and Solveig Gulbrandsen missed a penalty in the 61th minute.

Germany were European Champions

UEFA EUROPEAN WOMEN'S CHAMPIONSHIP
EURO 2017

For the first time there were 4 groups and the number 1 and 2 of each group proceed to the quarter-finals. All matches were played in the Netherlands.
After 6 tournaments with winner Germany, there was a different champion.
The host country Netherlands won there first trophy ever in history.
Since this tournament there was a 4th substitute in the extra time allowed.

GROUP A

16.07.2017   Stadion Galgenwaard, Utrecht: Netherlands – Norway 1-0 (0-0).

NETHERLANDS: Sari VAN VEENENDAAL, Desiree VAN LUNTEREN, Mandy VAN DEN BERG (79' Stefanie VAN DER GRAGT), Kika VAN ES, Anouk DEKKER, Sherida SPITSE, Daniëlle VAN DE DONK (90' Jill ROORD), Jackie GROENEN, Shanice VAN DE SANDEN (76' Lineth BEERENSTEYN), Vivianne MIEDEMA, Lieke MARTENS. (Coach: Sarina WIEGMAN).

NORWAY: Ingrid HJELMSETH, Ingrid MOE WOLD, Maria THORISDOTTIR, Maren MJELDE, Elise THORSNES, Nora HOLSTAD BERGE, Ingrid SCHJELDERUP (75' Guro REITEN), Frida MAANUM (57' Ingvild ISAKSEN), Caroline GRAHAM HANSEN, Ada STOLSMO HEGERBERG, Kristine HEGLAND-MINDE (66' Emilie HAAVI). (Coach: Martin SJÖGREN).

Referee: Stéphanie FRAPPART (FRA)   Attendance: 21,732.

Goal: Shanice VAN DE SANDEN 1-0.

Yellow Cards: Jackie GROENEN, Ada STOLSMO HEGERBERG.

16.07.2017   De Vijverberg, Doetinchem: Denmark – Belgium 1-0 (1-0).

DENMARK: Stina PETERSEN, Line RØDDIK, Janni ARNTH, Simone SØRENSEN, Theresa NIELSEN, Sanne TROELSGAARD-NIELSEN, Katrine VEJE, Line JENSEN, Nadia NADIM (71' Fredrikke THØGERSEN), Pernille HARDER, Stine LARSEN (60' Maja KILDEMOES). (Coach: Nils NIELSEN).

BELGIUM: Justin ODEURS, Davina PHILTJENS (87' Yana DANIELS), Heleen JACQUES, Maud COUTEREELS, Tine DE CAIGNY, Julie BIESMANS (82' Jana CORYN), Elke VAN GORP (62' Davinia VANMECHELEN), Lenie ONZIA, Tessa WULLAERT, Aline ZELER, Janice CAYMAN. (Coach: Ives SERNEELS).

Referee: Kateryna MONZUL (UKR)   Attendance: 5,000.

Goal: 6' Sanne TROELSGAARD-NIELSEN 1-0.

Yellow Cards: Line RØDDIK, Theresa NIELSEN, Nadia NADIM, Maja KILDEMOES, Davina PHILTJENS.

20.07.2017   Rat Verlegh, Breda: Norway – Belgium 0-2 (0-0).

NORWAY: Ingrid HJELMSETH, Ingrid MOE WOLD (46' Anja SØNSTEVOLD), Maren MJELDE, Elise THORSNES (75' Emilie HAAVI), Nora HOLSTAD BERGE, Ingrid SCHJELDERUP (79' Lisa-Marie KARLSENG UTLAND), Andrine STOLSMO HEGERBERG, Ingrid SPORD, Caroline GRAHAM HANSEN, Ada STOLSMO HEGERBERG, Kristine HEGLAND-MINDE. (Coach: Martin SJÖGREN).

BELGIUM: Justin ODEURS, Davina PHILTJENS (76' Jana CORYN), Heleen JACQUES, Maud COUTEREELS, Tine DE CAIGNY, Laura DELOOSE, Elke VAN GORP (88' Yana DANIELS), Lenie ONZIA, Tessa WULLAERT, Aline ZELER, Janice CAYMAN (90' Julie BIESMANS). (Coach: Ives SERNEELS).

Referee: Monika MULARCZYK (POL)   Attendance: 8,477.

Goals: 59' Elke VAN GORP 0-1, 67' Janice CAYMAN 0-2.

Yellow Cards: Anja SØNSTEVOLD, Heleen JACQUES, Aline ZELER.

20.07.2017   Het Kasteel, Rotterdam: Netherlands – Denmark 1-0 (1-0).

NETHERLANDS: Sari VAN VEENENDAAL, Desiree VAN LUNTEREN, Mandy VAN DEN BERG (53' Stefanie VAN DER GRAGT), Kika VAN ES, Anouk DEKKER, Sherida SPITSE, Daniëlle VAN DE DONK, Jackie GROENEN, Shanice VAN DE SANDEN (88' Lineth BEERENSTEYN), Vivianne MIEDEMA, Lieke MARTENS (78' Renate JANSEN). (Coach: Sarina WIEGMAN).

DENMARK: Stina PETERSEN, Simone SØRENSEN, Theresa NIELSEN, Mie JANS, Cecilie SANDVEJ, Nanna CHRISTIANSEN (64' Maja KILDEMOES), Sanne TROELSGAARD-NIELSEN, Katrine VEJE (69' Stine LARSEN), Line JENSEN, Nadia NADIM, Pernille HARDER. (Coach: Nils NIELSEN).

Referee: Riem HUSSEIN (GER)   Attendance: 10,599.

Goal: 20' Sherida SPITSE 1-0 (p).

Yellow Cards: Sanne TROELSGAARD-NIELSEN, Simone SØRENSEN, Maja KILDEMOES.

24.07.2017   Koning Willem II stadion, Tilburg: Belgium – Netherlands 1-2 (0-1).

BELGIUM: Justin ODEURS, Davina PHILTJENS, Heleen JACQUES, Maud COUTEREELS (46' Davinia VANMECHELEN), Tine DE CAIGNY, Laura DELOOSE, Elke VAN GORP (57' Jana CORYN), Lenie ONZIA (76' Yana DANIELS), Tessa WULLAERT, Aline ZELER, Janice CAYMAN. (Coach: Ives SERNEELS).

NETHERLANDS: Sari VAN VEENENDAAL, Stefanie VAN DER GRAGT, Kika VAN ES, Anouk DEKKER, Liza VAN DER MOST, Sherida SPITSE, Daniëlle VAN DE DONK (75' Kelly ZEEMAN), Jackie GROENEN (80' Jill ROORD), Shanice VAN DE SANDEN, Vivianne Miedema (86' Vanity LEWERISSA), Lieke MARTENS. (Coach: Sarina WIEGMAN).

Referee: Bibiana STEINHAUS (GER)   Attendance: 12,697.

Goals: 27' Sherida SPITSE 0-1 (p), 59' Tessa WULLAERT 1-1, 74' Lieke MARTENS 1-2.

Yellow Cards: Laura DELOOSE, Stefanie VAN DER GRAGT, Anouk DEKKER, Daniëlle VAN DE DONK, Vivianne MIEDEMA.

24.07.2017   De Adelaarshorst, Deventer: Norway – Denmark 0-1 (0-1).

NORWAY: Ingrid HJELMSETH, Ingrid MOE WOLD, Maria THORISDOTTIR, Maren MJELDE, Nora HOLSTAD BERGE, Ingrid SCHJELDERUP (56' Frida MAANUM), Ingrid SPORD (79' Lisa-Marie KARLSENG UTLAND), Guro REITEN, Caroline GRAHAM HANSEN, Ada STOLSMO HEGERBERG, Kristine HEGLAND-MINDE. (Coach: Martin SJÖGREN).

DENMARK: Stina PETERSEN, Line RØDDIK, Simone SØRENSEN, Theresa NIELSEN, Sanne TROELSGAARD-NIELSEN, Katrine VEJE (90' Nanna CHRISTIANSEN), Frederikke THØGERSEN (78' Nicoline SØRENSEN), Line JENSEN, Nadia NADIM (81' Cecilie SANDVEJ), Pernille HARDER, Stine LARSEN. (Coach: Nils NIELSEN).

Referee: Stéphanie FRAPPART (FRA)   Attendance: 5,885.

Goal: 5' Katrine VEJE 0-1.

Yellow Card: Maren MJELDE.

Caroline Graham Hansen missed a penalty in the 44th minute.

FINAL STANDINGS

1.	NETHERLANDS	3	3	0	0	4 - 1	9
2.	DENMARK	3	2	0	1	2 - 1	6
3.	BELGIUM	3	1	0	2	3 - 3	3
4.	NORWAY	3	0	0	3	0 - 4	0

GROUP B

17.07.2017   Het Kasteel, Rotterdam: Italy – Russia 1-2 (0-2).

ITALY: Chiara MARCHITELLI, Cecilia SALVAI, Sara GAMA (27' Linda TUCCERI CIMINI), Elena LINARI, Elisa BARTOLI, Daniela STRACCHI, Alia GUAGNI (71' Barbara BONANSEA), Manuela GIUGLIANO, Marta CARISSIMI (62' Cristiana GIRELLI), Melania GABBIADINI, Ilaria MAURO.   (Coach: Antonio CABRINI).

RUSSIA: Tatyana SHCHERBAK, Nastalya SOLODKAYA, Anna KOZHNIKOVA, Daria MAKARENKO, Elvira ZIYASTINOVA, Anna CHOLOVYAGA (59' Ekaterina PANTYUKHINA), Nadezhda SMIRNOVA, Ekaterina SOCHNEVA (90' Marina KISKONEN), Margarita CHERNOMYRDINA, Elena MOROZOVA, Elena DANILOVA (75' Nadezhda KARPOVA).   (Coach: Elena FOMINA).

Referee: Jana ADÁMKOVÁ (CZE)   Attendance: 669.

Goals: 9' Elena DANILOVA 0-1, 26' Elena MOROZOVA 0-2, 88' Ilaria MAURO 1-2.

Yellow Cards: Elena LINARI, Elisa BARTOLI, Tatyana SHCHERBAK.

17.07.2017   Rat Verlegh, Breda: Germany – Sweden 0-0.

GERMANY: Almuth SCHULT, Josephine HENNING, Babett PETER, Kristin DEMANN, Carolin SIMON, Anna BLÄSSE (73' Leonie MAIER), Dzsenifer MAROZSÁN, Sara DÄBRITZ, Svenja HUTH (39' Mandy ISLACKER), Lina MAGULL, Anja MITTAG (65' Hasret KAYIKCI). (Coach: Steffi JONES).

SWEDEN: Hedvig LINDAHL, Jonna ANDERSSON (87' Magdalena ERIKSSON), Linda SEMBRANT, Nilla FISCHER, Jessica SAMUELSSON, Lisa DAHLKVIST, Caroline SEGER, Olivia SCHOUGH (56' Elin RUBENSSON), Lotta SCHELIN, Kosovare ASLLANI, Fridolina ROLFÖ (56' Stina BLACKSTENIUS). (Coach: Pia SUNDHAGE).

Referee: Katalin KULCSÁR (HUN)   Attendance: 9,276.

Yellow Card: Lina MAGULL.

21.07.2017   De Adelaarshorst, Deventer: Sweden – Russia 2-0 (1-0).

SWEDEN: Hedvig LINDAHL, Linda SEMBRANT, Nilla FISCHER, Magdalena ERIKSSON, Jessica SAMUELSSON, Lisa DAHLKVIST (63' Hanna FOLKESSON), Caroline SEGER, Olivia SCHOUGH (46' Fridolina ROLFÖ), Lotta SCHELIN, Kosovare ASLLANI, Stina BLACKSTENIUS (73' Pauline HAMMARLUND). (Coach: Pia SUNDHAGE).

RUSSIA: Tatyana SHCHERBAK, Nastalya SOLODKAYA, Anna KOZHNIKOVA, Daria MAKARENKO, Elvira ZIYASTINOVA, Anna CHOLOVYAGA, Nadezhda SMIRNOVA, Ekaterina SOCHNEVA (81' Marina KISKONEN), Margarita CHERNOMYRDINA (66' Marina FEDOROVA), Elena MOROZOVA, Elena DANILOVA (73' Nadezhda KARPOVA). (Coach: Elena FOMINA).

Referee: Stéphanie FRAPPART (FRA)   Attendance: 5,764.

Goals: 22' Lotta SCHELIN 1-0, 52' Stina BLAKCSTENIUS 2-0.

Yellow Cards: Magdalena ERIKSSON, Ekaterina SOCHNEVA, Elena MOROZOVA.

21.07.2017   Koning Willem II stadion, Tilburg: Germany – Italy 2-1 (1-1).

GERMANY: Almuth SCHULT, Josephine HENNING (46' Kathrin HENDRICH), Leonie MAIER, Babett PETER, Kristin DEMANN, Isabel KERSCHOWSKI, Dzsenifer MAROZSÁN, Sara DÄBRITZ, Mandy ISLACKER (79' Lena PETERMANN), Anja MITTAG, Linda DALLMANN (88' Lina MAGULL).   (Coach: Steffi JONES).

ITALY: Laura GIULIANI, Cecilia SALVAI, Elena LINARI, Elisa BARTOLI, Daniela STRACCHI, Alia GUAGNI, Barbara BONANSEA, Valentina CERNOIA (73' Linda TUCCERI CIMINI), Marta CARISSIMI, Melania GABBIADINI (84' Daniela SABATINO), Ilaria MAURO (45' Cristiana GIRELLI).   (Coach: Antonio CABRINI).

Referee: Kateryna MONZUL (UKR)   Attendance: 7,108.

Goals: 19' Josephine HENNING 1-0, 29' Ilaria MAURO 1-1, 67' Babett PETER 2-1 (p).

Yellow Cards: Daniela STRACCHI, Marta CARISSIMI.

Red card: 69' Elisa BARTOLI.

25.07.2017   Stadion Galgenwaard, Utrecht: Russia – Germany 0-2 (0-1).

RUSSIA: Tatyana SHCHERBAK, Nastalya SOLODKAYA, Anna KOZHNIKOVA, Daria MAKARENKO (28' Ekaterina MOROZOVA), Elvira ZIYASTINOVA, Anna CHOLOVYAGA, Nadezhda SMIRNOVA (46' Marina FEDOROVA), Ekaterina SOCHNEVA, Margarita CHERNOMYRDINA (63' Nadezhda KARPOVA), Elena MOROZOVA, Elena DANILOVA.   (Coach: Elena FOMINA).

GERMANY: Almuth SCHULT, Babett PETER, Kristin DEMANN, Carolin SIMON, Anna BLÄSSE, Lena GOESSLING, Dzsenifer MAROZSÁN, Sara DÄBRITZ (68' Lina MAGULL), Sara DOORSOUN, Mandy ISLACKER (46' Hasret KAYIKCI), Anja MITTAG (75' Tabea KEMME).   (Coach: Steffi JONES).

Referee: Monika MULARCZYK (POL)   Attendance: 6,458.

Goals: 10' Babett PETER 0-1, 56' Dzsenifer MAROZSÁN 0-2 (p).

Yellow Cards: Anna KOZHNIKOVA.

25.07.2017   De Vijverberg, Doetinchem: Sweden – Italy 2-3 (1-2).

SWEDEN: Hedvig LINDAHL, Jonna ANDERSSON, Linda SEMBRANT, Magdalena ERIKSSON, Hanna FOLKESSON, Caroline SEGER (46' Lisa DAHLKVIST), Olivia SCHOUGH (79' Julia SPETSMARK), Elin RUBENSSON, Lotta SCHELIN, Kosovare ASLLANI (46' Fridolina ROLFÖ), Stina BLACKSTENIUS. (Coach: Pia SUNDHAGE).

ITALY: Laura GIULIANI, Elena LINARI, Linda TUCCERI CIMINI (60' Manuela GIUGLIANO), Federica DI CRISCIO, Daniela STRACCHI, Alia GUAGNI, Martina ROSUCCI (84' Marta CARISSIMI), Barbara BONANSEA, Aurora GALLI, Melania GABBIADINI, Daniela SABATINO (77' Cristiana GIRELLI). (Coach: Antonio CABRINI).

Referee: Esther STAUBLI (SUI)   Attendance: 5,203.

Goals: 4' Daniela SABATINO 0-1, 14' Lotta SCHELIN 1-1 (p), 37' Daniela SABATINO 1-2, 47' Stina BLACKSTENIUS 2-2, 85' Cristiana GIRELLI 2-3.

Yellow Cards: Linda TUCCERI CIMINI, Federica DI CRISCIO.

FINAL STANDINGS

1.	GERMANY	3	2	1	0	4 - 1	7
2.	SWEDEN	3	1	1	1	4 - 3	4
3.	RUSSIA	3	1	0	2	2 - 5	3
4.	ITALY	3	1	0	2	5 - 6	3

GROUP C

18.07.2017   De Adelaarshorst, Deventer: Austria – Switzerland 1-0 (1-0).

AUSTRIA: Manuela ZINSBERGER, Katharina SCHIECHTL (77' Viktoria SCHNADERBECK), Carina WENNINGER, Virginia KIRCHBERGER, Sarah ZADRAZIL, Sarah PUNTIGAM, Verena ASCHAUER, Nina BURGER, Nicole BILLA (83' Viktoria PINTHER), Laura FEIERSINGER, Lisa MAKAS (39' Nadine PROHASKA). (Coach: Dominik THALHAMMER).

SWITZERLAND: Gaëlle THALMANN, Noelle MARITZ, Rahel KIWIC, Caroline ABBÉ (57' Vanessa BERNAUER), Martina MOSER, Lara DICKENMANN, Lia WÄLTI, Géraldine REUTELER (62' Jana BRUNNER), Ana-Maria CRNOGORČEVIĆ, Ramona BACHMANN, Fabienne HUMM (57' Eseosa AIGBOGUN). (Coach: Martina VOSS-TECKLENBURG).

Referee: Bibiana STEINHAUS (GER)   Attendance: 4,781.

Goal: 15' Nina Burger 1-0.

Yellow Cards: Virginia KIRCHBERGER, Nina BURGER, Caroline ABBÉ.

Red card: 60' Rahel KIWIC.

18.07.2017   Koning Willem II stadion, Tilburg: France – Iceland 1-0 (0-0).

FRANCE: Sarah BOUHADDI, Wendie RENARD, Laura GEORGES, Jessica HOUARA D'HOMMEAUX, Sakina KARCHAOUI, Amandine HENRY, Camille ABILY, Élise BUSSAGLIA (64' Gaëtane THINEY), Clarisse LE BIHAN (42' Kadidiatou DIANI), Eugénie LE SOMMER, Élodie THOMIS (78' Marie-Laure DELIE). (Coach: Olivier ECHOUAFNI).

ICELAND: Gudbjörg GUNNARSDÓTTIR, Sif ATLADÓTTIR, Ingibjörg SIGURDARDÓTTIR, Glódis VIGGÓSDÓTTIR, Hallbera GISLADÓTTIR, Gunnhildur Yrsa JÓNSDÓTTIR, Sara Björk GUNNARSDÓTTIR, Sigridur Lára GARDARSDÓTTIR (76' Harpa PORSTEINSDÓTTIR), Dagný BRYNJARSDÓTTIR, Agla Maria ALBERTSDÓTTIR (61' Katrin ASBJÖRNSDÓTTIR), Fanndis FRIDRIKSDÓTTIR (82' Elin Metta JENSEN). (Coach: Freyr ALEXANDERSSON).

Referee: Carina VITULANO (ITA)   Attendance: 5,000.

Goals: 86' Eugénie LE SOMMER 1-0 (p).

Red cards: Wendie RENARD, Agla Maria ALBERTSDÓTTIR, Sandra SIGURDARDÓTTIR.

22.07.2017   De Vijverberg, Doetinchem: Iceland – Switzerland 1-2 (1-1).

ICELAND: Gudbjörg GUNNARSDÓTTIR, Sif ATLADÓTTIR, Ingibjörg SIGURDARDÓTTIR, Glódis VIGGÓSDÓTTIR, Hallbera GISLADÓTTIR, Gunnhildur Yrsa JÓNSDÓTTIR (83' Hólmfridur MAGNÚSDÓTTIR), Sara Björk GUNNARSDÓTTIR, Sigridur Lára GARDARSDÓTTIR (88' Harpa PORSTEINSDÓTTIR), Dagný BRYNJARSDÓTTIR, Katrin ASBJÖRNSDÓTTIR (66' Agla Maria ALBERTSDÓTTIR), Fanndis FRIDRIKSDÓTTIR. (Coach: Freyr ALEXANDERSSON).

SWITZERLAND: Gaëlle THALMANN, Jana BRUNNER, Noelle MARITZ, Martina MOSER (56' Eseosa AIGBOGUN), Cinzia ZEHNDER, Lara DICKENMANN, Lia WÄLTI, Vanessa BERNAUER, Vanessa BÜRKI (76' Fabienne HUMM), Ana-Maria CRNOGORČEVIĆ, Ramona BACHMANN (90' Rachel RINAST). (Coach: Martina VOSS-TECKLENBURG).

Referee: Ekaterina PUSTOVOITOVA (RUS)   Attendance: 5,647.

Goals: 33' Fanndis FRIDRIKSDÓTTIR 1-0, 43' Lara DICKENMANN 1-1, 52' Ramona BACHMANN 1-2.

Yellow Cards: Gunnhildur Yrsa JÓNSDÓTTIR, Lara DICKENMANN.

22.07.2017   Stadion Galgenwaard, Utrecht: France – Austria 1-1 (0-1).

FRANCE: Sarah BOUHADDI, Éve PERISSET, Wendie RENARD, Jessica HOUARA D'HOMMEAUX (64' Sakina KARCHAOUI), Griedge MBOCK BATHY, Amandine HENRY, Élise BUSSAGLIA (78' Camille ABILY), Gaëtane THINEY (71' Kadidiatou DIANI), Garce GEYORO, Eugénie LE SOMMER, Marie-Laure DELIE.
(Coach: Olivier ECHOUAFNI).

AUSTRIA: Manuela ZINSBERGER, Katharina SCHIECHTL, Carina WENNINGER, Viktoria SCHNADERBECK, Virginia KIRCHBERGER, Sarah PUNTIGAM, Verena ASCHAUER, Nina BURGER (75' Viktoria PINTHER), Nicole BILLA (85' Jasmin EDER), Laura FEIERSINGER, Lisa MAKAS (69' Nadine PROHASKA).
(Coach: Dominik THALHAMMER).

Referee: Jana ADÁMKOVÁ (CZE)   Attendance: 4,387.

Goals: 27' Lisa MAKAS 0-1, 51' Amandine HENRY 1-1.

Yellow Cards: Jessica HOUARA D'HOMMEAUX, Laura FEIERSINGER.

26.07.2017   Rat Verlegh, Breda: Switzerland – France 1-1 (1-0).

SWITZERLAND: Gaëlle THALMANN, Noelle MARITZ, Rahel KIWIC, Martina MOSER (65' Viola CALLIGARIS), Cinzia ZEHNDER (79' Géraldine REUTELER), Lara DICKENMANN, Lia WÄLTI, Vanessa BERNAUER, Ana-Maria CRNOGORČEVIĆ, Ramona BACHMANN, Eseosa AIGBOGUN (79' Meriame TERCHOUN).
(Coach: Martina VOSS-TECKLENBURG).

FRANCE: Sarah BOUHADDI, Éve PERISSET, Wendie RENARD, Griedge MBOCK BATHY, Sakina KARCHAOUI, Amandine HENRY, Camille Abily (87' Gaëtane THINEY), Claire LAVOGEZ (71' Marie-Lauare DELIE), Graace GEYORO, Eugénie LE SOMMER, Kadidiatou DIANI (83' Jessica HOUARA D'HOMMEAUX.   (Coach: Olivier ECHOUAFNI).

Referee: Katalin KULCSÁR (HUN)   Attendance: 4,511.

Goals: 19' Ana-Maria CRNOGORČEVIĆ 1-0, 76' Camille ABILY 1-1.

Yellow Cards: Lara DICKENMANN, Vanessa BERNAUER, Viola CALLIGARIS, Wendie RENARD, Amandine HENRY.

Red card: 17' Éve PERISSET.

26.07.2017   Het Kasteel, Rotterdam: Iceland – Austria 0-3 (0-2).

ICELAND: Gudbjörg GUNNARSDÓTTIR, Sif ATLADÓTTIR, Glódis VIGGÓSDÓTTIR, Hallbera GISLADÓTTIR, Anna Björk KRISTJÁNSDÓTTIR, Hólmfridur MAGNÚSDÓTTIR (51' Gunnhildur Yrsa JÓNSDÓTTIR), Sara Björk GUNNARSDÓTTIR, Dagný BRYNJARSDÓTTIR, Harpa PORSTEINSDÓTTIR (71' Berglind PORVALDSDÓTTIR), Agla Maria ALBERTSDÓTTIR (83' Sandra JESSEN), Fanndis FRIDRIKSDÓTTIR. (Coach: Freyr ALEXANDERSSON).

AUSTRIA: Manuela ZINSBERGER, Katharina SCHIECHTL, Carina WENNINGER, Virginia KIRCHBERGER, Sarah ZADRAZIL (72' Viktoria SCHNADERBECK), Sarah PUNTIGAM, Verena ASCHAUER, Nina BURGER, Nicole BILLA (86' Stefanie ENZINGER), Laura FEIERSINGER, Lisa MAKAS (56' Nadine PROHASKA). (Coach: Dominik THALHAMMER).

Referee: Riem HUSSEIN (GER)   Attendance: 4,352.

Goals: 36' Sarah ZADRAZIL 0-1, 44' Nina BURGER 0-2, 89' Stefanie ENZINGER 0-3.

Yellow Cards: Anna Björk KRISTJÁNSDÓTTIR, Sarah ZADRAZIL.

FINAL STANDINGS

1.	AUSTRIA	3	2	1	0	5	- 1	7
2.	FRANCE	3	1	2	0	3	- 2	5
3.	SWITZERLAND	3	1	1	1	3	- 3	4
4.	ICELAND	3	0	0	3	1	- 6	0

GROUP D

19.07.2017   De Vijverberg, Doetinchem: Spain – Portugal 2-0 (2-0).

SPAIN: Sandra PAÑOS Garcia-Villamil, Marta TORREJÓN Moya, IRENE Paredes Hernández, Andrea PEREIRA Cejudo, Leila OUAHABI El Ouhabi (89' Maria Pilar LEÓN Cebrián), Amanda SAMPEDRO Bustos, ALEXIA Putellas Segura (81' BÁRBARA Latorre Viñals), Maria Victoria LOSADA Gómez, Silvia MESEGUER Bellido, Maria Francesca Caldentey Oliver MARIONA, Jenni HERMOSO Fuentes (65' Maria PAZ Vilas Dono). (Coach: Jorge VILDA).

PORTUGAL: Patricia Isabel Sousa Barros MORAIS, Silvia Marisa Garcia REBELO, Carole da Silva COSTA, Cláudia Teresa Pires NETO, Tatiana Vanessa Ferreira PINTO, Dolores Isabel Jácome SILVA, Vanessa MARQUES Malho, Ana Catarina Marques BORGES, Ana Cristina Oliveira LEITE (59' Carolina Ana Trindade Coruche MENDES), Diana Micaela Abreu de Sousa e SILVA (85' Laura José Ramos LUIS), Suzane Lira PIRES (71' Mélissa ANTUNES).   (Coach: Francisco NETO).

Referee: Pernilla LARSSON (SWE)   Attendance: 3,100.

Goals: 23' Maria Victoria LOSADA Gómez 1-0, 42' Amanda SAMPEDRO Bustos 2-0.

19.07.2017 Stadion Galgenwaard, Utrecht: England – Scotland 6-0 (3-0).

ENGLAND: Karen BARDSLEY, Lucy BRONZE, Demi STOKES, Steph HOUGHTON, Millie BRIGHT, Jill SCOTT, Jordan NOBBS, Jade MOORE, Jodie TAYLOR (59' Toni DUGGAN), Ellen WHITE (74' Karen CARNEY), Fran KIRBY (65' Nikita PARRIS). (Coach: Mark SAMPSON).

SCOTLAND: Gemma FAY, Vaila BARSLEY, Ifeoma DIEKE, Rachel CORSIE (76' Joanne LOVE), Frankie BROWN, Caroline WEIR, Leanne CRICHTON, Lisa EVANS, Chloe ARTHUR, Jane ROSS (63' Erin CUTHBERT), Fiona BROWN (46' Lana CLELLAND). (Coach: Anna SIGNEUL).

Referee: Esther STAUBLI (SUI)   Attendance: 5,578.

Goals: 11', 26' Jodie TAYLOR 1-0, 2-0, 32' Ellen WHITE 3-0, 53' Jodie TAYLOR 4-0, 87' Jordan NOBBS 5-0, 90' Toni DUGGAN 6-0.

Yellow Cards: Steph HOUGHTON, Jill SCOTT, Caroline WEIR.

23.07.2017 Het Kasteel, Rotterdam: Scotland – Portugal 1-2 (0-1).

SCOTLAND: Gemma FAY, Vaila BARSLEY, Ifeoma DIEKE, Rachel CORSIE, Rachel MCLAUCHLAN (82' Joanne LOVE), Kirsty SMITH, Caroline WEIR, Leanne CRICHTON, Lisa EVANS, Lana CLELLAND (54' Erin CUTHBERT), Fiona BROWN (67' Hayley LAUDER). (Coach: Anna SIGNEUL).

PORTUGAL: Patricia Isabel Sousa Barros MORAIS, Silvia Marisa Garcia REBELO, Carole da Silva COSTA, Cláudia Teresa Pires NETO, Tatiana Vanessa Ferreira PINTO, Dolores Isabel Jácome SILVA, Vanessa MARQUES Malho, Amanda Jaqueline DACOSTA (76' Suzane Lira PIRES), Ana Catarina Marques BORGES, Diana Micaela Abreu de Sousa e SILVA (90' Laura José Ramos LUIS), Caroline Ana Trindade Coruche MENDES (70' Ana Cristina Oliveira LEITE). (Coach: Francisco NETO).

Referee: Katalin KULCSÁR (HUN)   Attendance: 3,123.

Goals: 27' Carolina Ana Trindade Coruche MENDES 0-1, 68' Erin CUTHBERT 1-1, 72' Ana Cristina Oliveira LEITE 1-2.

Yellow Cards: Rachel CORSIE, Patricia Isabel Sousa Barros MORAIS, Silvia Marisa Garcia REBELO, Carole da Silva COSTA, Cláudia Teresa Pires NETO, Diana Micaela Abreu de Sousa e SILVA.

23.07.2017   Rat Verlegh, Breda: England – Spain 2-0 (1-0).

ENGLAND: Karen BARDSLEY, Lucy BRONZE, Demi STOKES, Steph HOUGHTON, Millie BRIGHT, Jill SCOTT, Jordan NOBBS, Jade MOORE, Jodie TAYLOR (89' Jo POTTER), Ellen WHITE (79' Toni DUGGAN), Fran KIRBY (69' Isobel CHRISTIANSEN). (Coach: Mark SAMPSON).

SPAIN: Sandra PAÑOS Garcia-Villamil, Marta TORREJÓN Moya, IRENE Paredes Hernández, Andrea PEREIRA Cejudo, Leila OUAHABI El Ouhabi (89' Virginia TORRECILLA Reyes), Amanda SAMPEDRO Bustos (89' BÁRBARA Latorre Viñals), ALEXIA Putellas Segura, Maria Victoria LOSADA Gómez (73' OLGA Garcia Pérez), Silvia MESEGUER Bellido, Marta CORREDERA Rueda, Jenni HERMOSO Fuentes. (Coach: Jorge VILDA).

Referee: Carina VITULANO (ITA)   Attendance: 4,879.

Goals: 2' Fran KIRBY 1-0, 85' Jodie TAYLOR 2-0.

Yellow Cards: IRENE Paredes Hernández, Andrea PEREIRA Cejudo.

27.07.2017   Koning Willem II Stadion, Tilburg: Portugal – England 1-2 (1-1).

PORTUGAL: Patricia Isabel Sousa Barros MORAIS, Silvia Marisa Garcia REBELO, Carole da Silva COSTA, Cláudia Teresa Pires NETO, Tatiana Vanessa Ferreira PINTO, Dolores Isabel Jácome SILVA, Mélissa ANTUNES, Ana Catarina Marques BORGES, Diana Micaela Abreu de Sousa e SILVA (87' Laura José Ramos LUIS), Caroline Ana Trindade Coruche MENDES (64' Ana Cristina Oliveira LEITE), Suzane Lira PIRES (79' Amanda Jaqueline DACOSTA).   (Coach: Francisco NETO).

ENGLAND: Siobhan CHAMBERLAIN, Jo POTTER, Laura BASSETT, Millie BRIGHT (60' Jordan NOBBS), Alex GREENWOOD, Alex SCOTT, Isobel CHRISTIANSEN, Fara WILLIAMS, Karen CARNEY, Nikita PARRIS, Toni DUGGAN (81' Demi STOKES). (Coach: Mark SAMPSON).

Referee: Kateryna MONZUL (UKR)   Attendance: 3,335.

Goals: 7' Toni DUGGAN 0-1, 17' Caroline Ana Trindade Coruche MENDES 1-1, 48' Nikita PARRIS 1-2.

Yellow Cards: Isobel CHRISTIANSEN, Fara WILLIAMS.

27.07.2017   De Adelaarshorst, Deventer: Scotland – Spain 1-0 (1-0).

SCOTLAND: Gemma FAY, Ifeoma DIEKE, Rachel CORSIE, Frankie BROWN, Leanne ROSS (46' Lana CLELLAND), Joanne LOVE (73' Fiona BROWN), Erin CUTHBERT, Caroline WEIR, Leanne CRICHTON, Lisa EVANS, Chloe ARTHUR. (Coach: Anna SIGNEUL).

SPAIN: Sandra PAÑOS Garcia-Villamil, Marta TORREJÓN Moya, IRENE Paredes Hernández, Andrea PEREIRA Cejudo, Leila OUAHABI El Ouhabi (56' Marta CORREDERA Rueda), Amanda SAMPEDRO Bustos, ALEXIA Putellas Segura, Maria Victoria LOSADA Gómez, Silvia MESEGUER Bellido, Maria Francesca Caldentey Oliver MARIONA (79' BÁRBARA Latorre Viñals), Jenni HERMOSO Fuentes (46' Maria PAZ Vilas Dono). (Coach: Jorge VILDA).

Referee: Jana ADÁMKOVÁ (CZE)   Attendance: 4,840.

Goal: 42' Caroline WEIR 1-0.

Yellow Cards: Gemma FAY, Frankie BROWN, Leila OUAHABI El Ouhabi.

FINAL STANDINGS

1.	ENGLAND	3	3	0	0	10	- 1	9
2.	SPAIN	3	1	0	2	2	- 3	3
3.	SCOTLAND	3	1	0	2	2	- 8	3
4.	PORTUGAL	3	1	0	2	3	- 5	32

QUARTER-FINALS

29.07.2017   De Vijverberg, Doetinchem: Netherlands – Sweden 2-0 (1-0).

NETHERLANDS: Sari VAN VEENENDAAL, Desiree VAN LUNTEREN, Stefanie VAN DER GRAGT (46' Mandy VAN DEN BERG), Kika VAN ES, Anouk DEKKER, Sherida SPITSE, Daniëlle VAN DE DONK, Jackie GROENEN, Shanice VAN DE SANDEN (76' Renate JANSEN), Vivianne Miedema, Lieke MARTENS (87' Lineth BEERENSTEYN). (Coach: Sarina WIEGMAN).

SWEDEN: Hedvig LINDAHL, Jonna ANDERSSON (81' Mimmi LARSSON), Linda SEMBRANT, Nilla FISCHER, Jessica SAMUELSSON, Lisa DAHLKVIST, Caroline SEGER, Lotta SCHELIN, Kosovare ASLLANI, Stina BLACKSTENIUS, Fridolina ROLFÖ (73' Hanna FOLKESSON). (Coach: Pia SUNDHAGE).

Referee: Bibiana STEINHAUS (GER)   Attendance: 11,106.

Goals: 33' Lieke MARTENS 1-0, 64' Vivianne MIEDEMA 2-0.

Yellow Cards: Jessica SAMUELSSON, Kosovare ASLLANI.

30.07.2017　　　Het Kasteel, Rotterdam: Germany – Denmark 1-2 (1-0).

GERMANY: Almuth SCHULT, Babett PETER, Kristin DEMANN (62' Mandy ISLACKER), Anna BLÄSSE, Isabel KERSCHOWSKI, Lena GOESSLING, Dzsenifer MAROZSÁN, Sara DÄBRITZ, Sara DOORSOUN (446' Lina MAGULL), Anja MITTAG, Linda DALLMANN (88' Lena PETERMANN). (Coach: Steffi JONES).

DENMARK: Stina PETERSEN, Line RØDDIK (69' Cecilie SANDVEJ), Simone SØRENSEN, Theresa NIELSEN, Maja KILDEMOES (66' Frederikke THØGERSEN), Sanne TROELSGAARD-NIELSEN, Katrine VEJE, Line JENSEN, Nadia NADIM, Pernille HARDER, Stine LARSEN. (Coach: Nils NIELSEN).

Referee: Katalin KULCSÁR (HUN)　　Attendance: 5,251.

Goals: 3' Isabel KERSCHOWSKI 1-0, 49' Nadia NADIM 1-1, 83' Theresa NIELSEN 1-2.

30.07.2017　　　Koning Willem II Stadion, Tilburg: Austria – Spain 0-0 (0-0, 0-0, 0-0).

AUSTRIA: Manuela ZINSBERGER, Katharina SCHIECHTL, Carina WENNINGER, Viktoria SCHNADERBECK, Sarah ZADRAZIL (110' Viktoria PINTHER), Sarah PUNTIGAM, Verena ASCHAUER, Nina BURGER, Nicole BILLA (81' Virginia KIRCHBERGER), Laura FEIERSINGER, Lisa MAKAS (42' Nadine PROHASKA). (Coach: Dominik THALHAMMER).

SPAIN: Sandra PAÑOS Garcia-Villamil, Marta TORREJÓN Moya, IRENE Paredes Hernández, Maria Pilar LEÓN Cebrián, Amanda SAMPEDRO Bustos, Victoria LOSADA Gómez (68' ALEXIA Putellas Segura), Silvia MESEGUER Bellido, Maria Francesca Caldentey Oliver MARIONA (56' OLGA Garcia Pérez), Marta CORREDERA Rueda, Maria PAZ Vilas Dono (112' Virginia TORRECILLA Reyes), BÁRBARA Latorre Viñals (76' Jenni HERMOSO Fuentes). (Coach: Jorge VILDA).

Referee: Stéphanie FRAPPART (FRA)　　Attendance: 3,488.

Yellow Cards: Carina WENNINGER, Verena ASCHAUER, Marta TORREJÓN Moya, Maria Pilar LEÓN Cebrián.

Austria won 5-3 on penalties.

Penalties: Laura FEIERSINGER 1-0, OLGA Garcia Pérez 1-1, Nina BURGER 2-1, Amanda SAMPEDRO Bustos 2-2, Verena ASCHAUER 3-2, Silvia MESEGUER Bellido missed, Viktoria PINTHER 4-2, Marta CORREDERA Rueda 4-3, Sarah PUNTIGAM 5-3.

30.07.2017   De Adelaarshorst, Deventer: England – France 1-0 (0-0).

ENGLAND: Karen BARDSLEY (75' Siobhan CHAMBERLAIN), Lucy BRONZE, Demi STOKES, Steph HOUGHTON, Millie BRIGHT, Jill SCOTT, Jordan NOBBS, Jade MOORE, Jodie TAYLOR, Ellen WHITE, Fran KIRBY.   (Coach: Mark SAMPSON).

FRANCE: Sarah BOUHADDI, Laura GEORGES, Jessica HOUARA D'HOMMEAUX, Griedge MBOCK BATHY, Sakina KARCHAOUI, Amandine HENRY, Camille ABILY (78' Claire LAVOGEZ), Grace GEYORO, Eugénie LE SOMMER, Marie-Laure DELIE (90' Clarisse LE BIHAN), Kadidiatou DIANI (65' Élodie THOMAS).
(Coach: Olivier ECHOUAFNI).

Referee: Esther STAUBLI (SUI)   Attendance: 6,283.

Goal: 60' Jodie TAYLOR 1-0.

Yellow Cards: Jill SCOTT, Jodie TAYLOR, Griedge MBOCK BATHY.

SEMI-FINALS

03.08.2017   Rat Verlegh, Breda: Denmark – Austria 0-0 (0-0, 0-0, 0-0).

DENMARK: Stina PETERSEN, Line RØDDIK (46' Cecilie SANDVEJ), Simone SØRENSEN, Theresa NIELSEN, Maja KILDEMOES (52' Frederikke THØGERSEN), Sanne TROELSGAARD-NIELSEN, Katrine VEJE (120' Nicoline SÖRENSEN), Line JENSEN (69' Sofie PEDERSEN), Nadia NADIM, Pernille HARDER, Stine LARSEN.
(Coach: Nils NIELSEN).

AUSTRIA: Manuela ZINSBERGER, Katharina SCHIECHTL, Carina WENNINGER, Viktoria SCHNADERBECK, Virginia KIRCHBERGER, Sarah ZADRAZIL, Sarah PUNTIGAM (91' Viktoria PINTHER), Verena ASCHAUER, Nina BURGER, Nicole BILLA (39' Nadine PROHASKA), Laura FEIERSINGER.   (Coach: Dominik THALHAMMER).

Referee: Kateryna MONZUL (UKR)   Attendance: 12,000.

Yellow Cards: Maja KILDEMOES, Pernille HARDER, Katharina SCHIECHTL, Sarah ZADRAZIL.

Sarah Puntigam missed a penalty in the 13th minute.

Denmark won 3-0 on penalties.

Penalties: Nadia NADIM 1-0, Laura FEIERSINGER missed, Pernille HARDER 2-0, Viktoria PINTHER missed, Sofie PEDERSEN missed, Verena ASCHAUER missed, Simone SØRENSEN 3-0.

03.08.2017   De Grolsch Veste, Enschede: Netherlands – England 3-0 (1-0).

NETHERLANDS: Sari VAN VEENENDAAL, Desiree VAN LUNTEREN, Stefanie VAN DER GRAGT (70' Kelly ZEEMAN), Kika VAN ES, Anouk DEKKER, Sherida SPITSE, Daniëlle VAN DE DONK (90' Jill ROORD), Jackie GROENEN, Shanice VAN DE SANDEN (89' Renate JANSEN), Vivianne Miedema, Lieke MARTENS.   (Coach: Sarina WIEGMAN).

ENGLAND: Siobhan CHAMBERLAIN, Lucy BRONZE, Demi STOKES, Steph HOUGHTON, Millie BRIGHT, Jordan NOBBS, Fara WILLIAMS (67' Toni DUGGAN), Jade MOORE (76' Karen CARNEY), Jodie TAYLOR, Ellen WHITE, Fran KIRBY.
(Coach: Mark SAMPSON).

Referee: Stéphanie FRAPPART (FRA)   Attendance: 27,093.

Goals: 22' Vivianne MIEDEMA 1-0, 62' Daniëlle VAN DE DONK 2-0,
90' Millie BRIGHT 3-0 (og).

Yellow Cards: Desiree VAN LUNTEREN, Daniëlle VAN DE DONK, Millie BRIGHT, Jade MOORE.

FINAL

06.08.2017   De Grolsch Veste, Enschede: Netherlands – Denmark 4-2 (2-2).

NETHERLANDS: Sari VAN VEENENDAAL, Desiree VAN LUNTEREN (57' Dominique JANSSEN), Stefanie VAN DER GRAGT, Kika VAN ES (90' Mandy VAN DEN BERG), Anouk DEKKER, Sherida SPITSE, Daniëlle VAN DE DONK, Jackie GROENEN, Shanice VAN DE SANDEN (90' Renate JANSEN), Vivianne Miedema, Lieke MARTENS.
(Coach: Sarina WIEGMAN).

DENMARK: Stina PETERSEN, Simone SØRENSEN (77' Line RØDDIK), Theresa NIELSEN, Cecilia SANDVEJ, Maja KILDEMOES (61' Frederikke THØGERSEN), Sanne TROELSGAARD-NIELSEN, Katrine VEJE, Sofie PEDERSEN (82' Nanna CHRISTIANSEN), Nadia NADIM, Pernille HARDER, Stine LARSEN.
(Coach: Nils NIELSEN).

Referee: Esther STAUBLI (SUI)   Attendance: 28,182.

Goals: 6' Nadia NADIM 0-1 (p), 10' Vivianne MIEDEMA 1-1, 28' Lieke MARTENS 2-1, 33' Pernille HARDER 2-2, 51' Sherida SPITSE 3-2, 89' Vivianne MIEDEMA 4-2.

Yellow Cards: Stefanie VAN DER GRAGT, Anouk DEKKER, Jackie GROENEN, Nadia NADIM.

Netherlands were European Champions

UEFA EUROPEAN WOMEN'S CHAMPIONSHIP

WINNERS BY YEAR

1984	SWEDEN
1987	NORWAY
1989	GERMANY
1991	GERMANY
1993	NORWAY
1995	GERMANY
1997	GERMANY
2001	GERMANY
2005	GERMANY
2009	GERMANY
2013	GERMANY
2017	NETHERLANDS

GOALS AND MATCHES BY YEAR

1984	14	6	2.33
1987	13	4	3.25
1989	36	12	3.00
1991	24	12	2.00
1993	34	12	2.83
1995	51	13	3.92
1997	35	15	2.33
2001	40	15	2.67
2005	50	15	3.33
2009	75	25	3.00
2013	56	25	2.24
2017	68	31	2.19

TOPSCORER(S) BY YEAR

Year	Player	Goals	Country
1984	Pia SUNDHAGE	3	SWEDEN
1987	Trude STENDAL	3	NORWAY
1989	Lena VIDEKULL	4	SWEDEN
	Sissel GRUDE	4	NORWAY
	Carolina MORACE	4	ITALY
1991	Heidi MOHR	7	GERMANY
1993	Carolina MORACE	5	ITALY
1995	Heidi MOHR	5	GERMANY
1997	Carolina MORACE	5	ITALY
2001	Claudia MÜLLER	3	GERMANY
	Sandra SMISEK	3	GERMANY
2005	Inka GRINGS	4	GERMANY
2009	Inka GRINGS	6	GERMANY
2013	Lotta SCHELIN	5	SWEDEN
2017	Jodie TAYLOR	5	ENGLAND

ATTENDANCES BY YEAR

Year	Total	Avg	Notes
1984	20,720	3,453	
1987	14,428	3,607	
1989	50,246	4,187	
1991	31,409	2,617	
1993	17,628	1,762	(10 matches instead of 12. Attendance of 2 matches unknown)
1995	37,845	2,911	
1997	35,697	2,745	(13 matches instead of 15. Attendance of 2 matches unknown)
2001	92,703	6,180	
2005	117,602	7,840	
2009	129,905	5,196	
2013	216,908	8,676	
2017	245,804	7,929	

WINNING COACHES BY YEAR

1984	Ulf LYFORS	SWEDEN
1987	Erling HOKSTAD	NORWAY
1989	Gero BISANZ	GERMANY
1991	Gero BISANZ	GERMANY
1993	Even PELLERUD	NORWAY
1995	Gero BISANZ	GERMANY
1997	Tina THEUNE	GERMANY
2001	Tina THEUNE	GERMANY
2005	Tina THEUNE	GERMANY
2009	Silvia NEID	GERMANY
2013	Silvia NEID	GERMANY
2017	Sarina WIEGMAN	NETHERLANDS

ALL-TIME TOPSCORERS

Carolina MORACE	18	ITALY
Heidi MOHR	16	GERMANY
Inka GRINGS	10	GERMANY
Birgit PRINZ	10	GERMANY
Lena VIDEKULL	9	SWEDEN
Lotta SCHELIN	8	SWEDEN
Anneli ANDELEN	6	SWEDEN
Hanna LJUNGBERG	6	SWEDEN
Pia SUNDHAGE	6	SWEDEN
Melania GABBIADINI	5	ITALY
Solveig GULBRANDSEN	5	NORWAY
Maren MEINERT	5	GERMANY
Silvia NEID	5	GERMANY
Marianne PETTERSEN	5	NORWAY
Jodie TAYLOR	5	ENGLAND
Bettina Wiegmann	5	GERMANY

ALL-TIME MATCHES

Doris FITSCHEN	25	GERMANY
Birgit PRINZ	25	GERMANY
Bettina WIEGMANN	23	GERMANY
Carolina MORACE	22	ITALY
Solveig GULBRANDSEN	20	NORWAY
Patrizia PANICO	19	ITALY
Hege RIISE	19	NORWAY
Katrine SØNDERGAARD PEDERSEN	19	DENMARK
Heidi STØRE	19	NORWAY
Kristin BENGTSSON	18	SWEDEN
Elisabeth LEIDINGE	18	SWEDEN
Linda MEDALEN	18	NORWAY
Antonella CARTA	17	ITALY
Federica D'ASTOLFO	17	ITALY
Ariane HINGST	17	GERMANY
Emma IOZZELLI	17	ITALY
Maren MEINERT	17	GERMANY
Anja MITTAG	17	GERMANY
Heidi MOHR	17	GERMANY
Silvia NEID	17	GERMANY
Sandrine SOUBEYRAND	17	FRANCE
Victoria SVENSSON	17	SWEDEN
Lena VIDEKULL	17	SWEDEN
Martina VOSS-TECKLENBURG	17	GERMANY

ALL-TIME REFEREES

Bibiana STEINHAUS	9	GER
Kateryna MONZUL	9	UKR
Dagmar DAMKOVÁ	7	CZE
Kirsi HEIKKINEN	7	FIN
Katalin KULCSÁR	7	HUN
Esther STAUBLI	7	SUI
Nicole PETIGNAT	6	SUI
Alexandra IHRINGOVÁ	5	ENG
Gyöngyi GAÁL	5	HUN
Jenny PALMQVIST	5	SWE
Cristina DORCIOMAN	5	ROM
Stéphanie FRAPPART	5	FRA
Katriina ELOVIRTA	4	FIN
Carina VITULANO	4	ITA
Eva OEDLUND	3	SWE
Wendy THOMS	3	ENG
Kari SEITZ	3	USA
Jana ADÁMKOVÁ	3	CZE
Eere AHO	2	FIN
Cornelius BAKKER	2	HOL
Michal LISTKIEWICZ	2	POL
Vibeke KARLSEN	2	NOR
Gitte NIELSEN	2	DEN
Christine FRAI	2	GER
Regina BELKSMA-KONINK	2	HOL
Rita RUIZ-TACORONTE	2	ESP
Bente SKOGVANG	2	NOR
Claudine BROHET	2	BEL
Elke FIELENBACH	2	GER
Natalia AVDONCHENKO	2	RUS
Teodora ALBON	2	ROM
Monika MULARCZYK	2	POL
Riem HUSSEIN	2	GER
Kevin O'SULLIVAN	1	IRL
Werner FÖCKLER	1	GER
Kaj NATRI	1	FIN
Rolf HAUGEN	1	NOR
Ignace GORIS	1	BEL
Eysteinn GUDMUNDSSON	1	ISL
Peter MIKKELSEN	1	DEN
Gudmundur HARALDSSON	1	ISL
Wolf-Günter WIESEL	1	GER
John LLOYD	1	WAL
Charles AGIUS	1	MLT
Ion CRACIUNESCU	1	ROM
José SILVA	1	POR
Charles GILSON	1	LUX

Brian HILL	1	ENG
Ivan GREGR	1	CZE
Carlos VALENTE	1	POR
Klaus PESCHEL	1	GER
Rodger GIFFORD	1	WAL
Jaap UILENBERG	1	HOL
Karl-Josef ASSENMACHER	1	GER
Guy GOETHALS	1	BEL
Andrew WADDELL	1	SCO
Michel GIRARD	1	FRA
Luben SPASOV	1	BUL
Roger PHILIPPI	1	LUX
Garcia DE LOZA	1	ESP
James MCCLUSKEY	1	SCO
Nemus DJURHUUS	1	FRO
Daniel RODUIT	1	SUI
Wojciech RUDY	1	POL
Gilles VEISSIÈRE	1	FRA
Gerd GRABHER	1	AUT
Léon SCHELINGS	1	BEL
José MENDES PRATA	1	POR
Frank MCDONALD	1	NIR
Plarent KOTHERJA	1	ALB
Anders FRISK	1	SWE
Dick JOL	1	HOL
Alfred WIESER	1	AUT
Timo KELTANEN	1	FIN
Luben ANGELOV	1	BUL
Fernand MEESE	1	BEL
Mateo BEUSAN	1	CRO
Gheorghe CONSTANTIN	1	ROM
István VADA	1	HUN
Herbert BARR	1	NIR
Richard O'HANLON	1	IRL
Sándor PILLER	1	HUN
Finn LAMBEK	1	DEN
Kostadin GERGINOV	1	BUL
Willie YOUNG	1	SCO
Ilkka KOHO	1	FIN
Cristina GOZZI	1	ITA
Floarea BABADAC	1	ROM
Silvia SPINELLI	1	ITA
Ekaterina PUSTOVOITOVA	1	RUS
Pernilla LARSSON	1	SWE

ALL-TIME COACHES

Even PELLERUD	18	NOR
Gero BISANZ	17	GER
Sergio GUENZA	17	ITA
Hope POWELL	15	ENG
Tina THEUNE	15	GER
Keld GANZTHORN	12	DEN
Marika DOMANSKI-LYFORS	13	SWE
Silvia NEID	12	GER
Bjarne BERNTSEN	10	NOR
Elisabeth LOISEL	9	FRA
Pia SUNDHAGE	9	SWE
Unknown	8	SWE
Bruno BINI	8	FRA
Ignacio QUEREDA	8	ESP
Kenneth HEINER-MØLLER	8	DEN
Unknown	7	ITA
Sigurdur EYJÓLFSSON	7	ISL
Antonio CABRINI	7	ITA
Martin REAGAN	6	ENG
Ulf LYFORS	6	SWE
Erling HOKSTAD	6	NOR
Yuriy BYSTRITSKIY	6	RUS
Nils NIELSEN	6	DEN
Sarina WIEGMAN	6	NET
Bengt SIMONSON	5	SWE
Vera PAUW	5	NET
Dominik THALHAMMER	5	AUT
Mark SAMPSON	5	ENG
Ted COPELAND	4	ENG
Unknown	4	ENG
Unknown	4	RUS
Poul HØJMOSE	4	DEN
Age STEEN	4	NOR
Michael KÄLD	4	FIN
Pietro GHEDIN	4	ITA
Thomas DENNERBY	4	SWE
Unknown	4	FIN
Steffi JONES	4	GER
Olivier ECHOUAFNI	4	FRA
Jorge VILDA	4	ESP
Jørgen HVIDEMOSE	3	DEN
Per-Mathias HØGMO	3	NOR
Carolina MORACE	3	ITA
Peter BONDE	3	DEN
Unknown	3	UKR
Igor SHALIMOV	3	RUS
Andrée JEGLERTZ	3	FIN

Roger REIJNERS	3	NET
Sergei LAVRENTYEV	3	RUS
Martin SJÖGREN	3	NCR
CERNEELS	3	BEL
Elena FOMINA	3	RUS
Freyr ALEXANDERSSON	3	ISL
Martina VOSS-TECKLENBURG	3	SUI
Francisco NETO	3	POR
Anna SIGNEUL	3	SCO
Flemming SCHULTZ	2	DEN
Ettore RECAGNI	2	ITA
Piet BUTER	2	NET
Aimé MIGNOT	2	FRA
Bert VAN LINGEN	2	NET
Jan DERKS	2	NET
Logi ÓLAFSSON	2	ISL
Unknown	2	CSSR
Unknown	2	HUN

ALL-TIME COUNTRIES

1.	Germany	48	37	8	3	109	- 26	119
2.	Norway	44	23	7	14	69	- 53	76
3.	Sweden	45	21	9	15	75	- 49	72
4.	Denmark	38	12	11	15	40	- 52	47
5.	Italy	40	12	8	20	50	- 67	44
6.	England	34	13	3	18	47	- 65	42
7.	France	23	8	7	8	30	- 33	31
8.	Netherlands	20	8	3	9	20	- 22	27
9.	Spain	12	3	3	6	10	- 14	12
10.	Finland	11	3	3	5	11	- 19	12
11.	Austria	5	2	3	0	5	- 1	9
12.	Russia	19	1	4	14	10	- 43	7
13.	Switzerland	3	1	1	1	3	- 3	4
14.	Iceland	12	1	1	10	6	- 23	4
15.	Belgium	3	1	0	2	3	- 3	3
16.	Portugal	3	1	0	2	3	- 5	3
17.	Ukraine	3	1	0	2	2	- 4	3
18.	Scotland	3	1	0	2	2	- 8	3
19.	CSSR	2	0	1	1	1	- 3	1
20.	Hungary	2	0	0	2	1	- 4	0